THE

Real
PREACHER'S
Wife

BY

DEBRA OWENS GOUDY

TRILOGY
PROFESSIONAL PUBLISHING MEETS POWERFUL PROMOTION

A wholly owned subsidary of TBN

The Real Preacher's Wife
Trilogy Christian Publishers A Wholly Owned Subsidiary of Trinity Broadcasting Network
2442 Michelle Drive Tustin, CA 92780

Rights Department, 2442 Michelle Drive, Tustin, CA 92780.
Trilogy Christian Publishing/TBN and colophon are trademarks of Trinity Broadcasting Network.
Cover design by: Debra Owens Goudy
For information about special discounts for bulk purchases, please contact Trilogy Christian Publishing.

Manufactured in the United States of America
10 9 8 7 6 5 4 3 2 1
Library of Congress Cataloging-in-Publication Data is available.
ISBN: 978-1-63769-896-9
E-ISBN: 978-1-63769-897-6

Dedication

This book is dedicated to my mother, Mrs Louise Owens, she was the Epitome of a Pastor's wife for 42 years until her death.

She was an Awesome Mother with a prayer life, her genuine love for the clergy in her calm words were always the same. There's more power in a backslidden preacher to send you to hell,keep your mouth off him. Her strength was in being an example to her children and many more that loved and adore her. This book is dedicated to her Legacy.

Table of Contents

Preface

If the Lord has led you to pick up this book, it is not by accident. The reason I feel more qualified to write this book is simple: I am a preacher's wife; my husband is a pastor. I come from a long line of clergy: my grandfather, my father, and my uncles. This has afforded me the ability to witness firsthand what actually takes place in our homes and churches.

It is my endeavor that after you have purchased this book and have read it, whether you are clergy or laymen, a deacon, an evangelist, a bishop, or the person next door, you will have a new reverence for the preacher's wife, thus honoring the man of God will come naturally.

This book is not to banish the preacher or criticize their office, but to open eyes and hearts to the realization that there is somebody else in that office with him and that she is no other than *the preacher's wife*.

Why Me?

I must start this book with my personal experience as a preacher's wife. For me, it started in August 1982; my husband and I had set a date to be married. We both grew up in the church as infants. I had adored him since the age of eight, but he never noticed me. Then, my dad left the church to help his brother's ministry; I was about twelve years of age. My husband and I didn't see each other again until I was seventeen years of age. One Sunday, my mother suggested we go to a revival, being spiritual babes; she said she wanted us in a fiery service where there were young people our age.

So we went, and I saw my husband coming up the stairs as I was going down to the lower level. He asked for my number and said he would call me later. I anxiously waited by the phone, and he called. We immediately hit it off. But there was one problem: I knew I wanted to marry him, but how? We had nothing between us. I was working at Arby's, and he was seeking employment and being fresh out of high school. Dating was not accepted in the church—not unless you were getting married. Well, we were. My husband wanted to get married right away. The Lord told him

I was his wife. We re-met in April and were married in August 1982.

I often say we had nothing but Jesus and each other. But I still would have married him later, but we didn't have that option. "No courting" was all you heard, "no dating"; everything was no. He gave up sports, which he was good at because you couldn't play ball. He was even scared to hold my hand, even after we were married. Many people told us to get married.

His mother was the only one that said to wait to prepare ourselves. Well, we had nothing but my bedroom with a twin-size bed. He moved into my parents' house, we lived upstairs and paid rent, twenty dollars a week.

My husband was a young junior deacon when I married him. One month after we were married, we were eighteen and nineteen years of age, and he became a young minister. Well, for me, my whole life changed. First of all, I grew up as a preacher's daughter, and of course, that's for another book.

But I did not want to be a preacher's wife. I wanted to be submissive, but I didn't understand why a preacher? Once again, my life, which was supposed to be full of joy, became oppressed by people and their expectations.

My clothing changed, my hair, no make-up, no designer stockings, no shoes with the toe out, no splits; everything was no. No see-through sleeve dresses or tops. The funny thing about it is our whole world changed around us. The wives changed, but the husbands didn't. Our conversations change, our company changes, yet it seems as though the person that's the closest to us pushes us away.

So, immediately, my name changed, my social security card changed, my status changed, my living arrangements changed. My identity flew out the window. My vocal cords took a vacation.

If you spoke too much, you were being rebellious; I guess that was me with questions.

My appearance I didn't even recognize, not to mention my wardrobe! After all, they told me, "Baby, you're a preacher's wife now! He's no longer yours, he's everybody's; you must learn to share." Well, about that time, I was about to go into cardiac arrest.

I'd been stripped to serve. We had lived in the poorest conditions and were even on welfare. Yet, I was still the preacher's wife. I can't even explain all the things we had to endure to get us where we are today.

After thirty-nine years of marriage, five children, and nine grandchildren, it was not so easy, yet people think it's a glamorous job. Your role isn't much more than that of a pulpit flower.

In the next few chapters, I will unfold the job that the preacher's wife has had to endure. Then we'll see if you see what I see.

I want to dedicate this book to all the women that have made untold sacrifices that have been kept silent for years. Due to protocol. You are remarkable women that should be cherished. Many of you have been my examples. I honor you in this book. You are the virtuous women of God. I heard a quote about this recently, "Well-behaved women rarely make history."

This book is also dedicated to my mother, who passed away. Mother Louise Owens. To her life and legacy of righteous living and ministry and children. I am honored to have been her daughter, the real preacher's wife that rests now in the arms of Jesus, and I am privileged to share records from many other women. Tell your pastor's wife how much she means to you before she closes her eyes on this side of heaven.

Silence of the Lambs

Back in the day, the average preacher's wife had no outward privileges, only behind the scenes in the church, unlike today, when we have co-pastors, assistant women pastors, and so on.

If your husband was a clergyman, you were in the background. If you wanted to speak, you spoke in the testimony service with everybody else. As a matter of fact, clergy were taught to give more respect to others than to their wives. Most places had church mothers, and they would be given special space to exhort the church! But not the preacher's wife who would be holding a sewing circle, shut-ins (the real ones), bake sales, cleaning the church, killing, cleaning, then cooking the chicken, selling, and delivering. She would also counsel and pray for the church body, clean toilets and the church, and mop. She'd hold special programs for the pastor like she was a visitor. Prepare her own family for church, cook Sunday's dinner. Saturday night, get everybody's clothes out for Sunday. Cook Sunday breakfast for their children because they fasted until after service, help her husband find his ties and shoes (and brain, if necessary), and make it to church on time!

Then, when he'd finally mount the pulpit and start giving honor to whom honor is due, he'd forget to honor his own wife. "Oh, I forgot: and to my own wife…" Most proceed straight to the scripture, never considering honoring her.

I never understood that.

The wife is the one that makes your engine run smooth; how could you forget the oil?

Many preachers' wives have endured shame and burnout. The pastor sets the tone for respect for his wife. The church family will realize that you are a team together, and people won't see you any different. I'm sorry, I haven't seen the glamour yet. After all that she's endured on her regular job and at home, she's also a mother who seems like the feeble in the church, in which not everyone is needy, just most of them.

"Now we exhort you, brethren, warn them that are unruly, comfort the feebleminded, support the weak, be patient toward all *men*" (1 Thessalonians 5:14, NKJV).

A true preacher's wife guides her home as well as the ministry.

God seems to give these women strength and courage;

even when they are weak and sick in their own bodies, they yet were faithful. We can never step over these women just to get to their husbands. Preachers' wives have suffered. God gives them discernment. I think sometimes they are surprised at what God shows them about the flock. Many times, they endured breakdowns in their own homes and have not been able to talk to anyone about how the pastor is really treating them. They have problems just like any other married couple. Who do they have to counsel them? God has to intervene.

You may say, my pastor's wife is foolish, she's this or that, but ask yourself a question; very few start out that way.

Maybe somewhere along the line, her trust was violated; we're talking about humans here. I'm sure she wants to be sweet and kind but can't recover from how some people really hurt her and, yes, falsely accuse her. She, too, needs to be loved. It has taken years for the preachers' wives to gain the status in the church that they have now. Working side by side with their husbands, many times leading while bleeding. It has always been the will of God for us to be by their side.

When my husband started pastoring, he named me his

co-pastor. I did not want it, mostly due to the tradition of the church, but I work in that office because, after all the mistakes and failures we've made in our own lives, nobody could assist him like I could.

So, when you see a preacher's wife and you desire what she has, be very, very careful; you don't know what they have been through with that man to wear that fur coat, big diamond ring, and whatever they possess. Be careful. The scripture says, "Thou shalt not covet thy neighbor's [anything]"; get your own!

They deserve what they have, believe me. I remember an incident when my pastor had given his wife a birthday party. She, myself, and another lady were in the restroom. The other lady said to my then pastor's wife, "You think you're something because he gave you a party!" Immediately, I didn't allow my pastor's wife to gather her thoughts; I spoke and told her she was worth whatever she deserves, and she should get it! Then I told the other lady that she didn't suffer with that man—the wife did. I was very angry about that. This happened before we pastored, many years ago.

But guess what? Now that same lady is a bishop's wife, and she is persecuted by her members. Boy, keep your mouth shut. That lady knew better, but the devil in her made her verbalize it anyway. I realized that I love the clergy, and I wasn't going to be a partaker.

So I stood for what I knew was right, and my preacher's wife agreed; it has taken them far too long to have a voice in our local assemblies. We must love and support their wives as much as we want to support their husbands **(Romans 13:7, KJV)**.

Sharing the Ministry

"For this cause shall a man leave his father and mother, and shall be joined unto his wife, and they two shall be one flesh" (Ephesians 5:31).

Once again, many modern-day clergy share the ministry with their spouses. But I remember when the preacher's wife was allowed to have remarks—it was just before dismissal of service. And even then, her words were sifted as flour many times en route home. The preacher himself would comment, saying, "You shouldn't have said this or that or reacted that way."

This made it very hard to fit in anywhere. God forbid if God wanted to spontaneously use the preacher's wife's gift; it would have to be planned at least a month in advance for her to be able to mount and minister in the same capacity as her husband. And if they were anointed highly, he would find fault and give her more Sundays of silence.

I really admire the knowledge that most clergy have today. They allow their wife to be the closest person sitting next to them, and if God wants to use her spontaneously, He can, without the pastor feeling threatened. Because they complete each other on the same team.

The only other problem some still struggle with is that when God uses the preacher's wife, they find it hard to tell her, "Honey, God really used you today. I'm proud of you." Her attack is real too. Instead, they will say nothing, and sometimes that hurts worse than when they silence you. But God wants us to support and admonish each other. We help each other to do good. **Nevertheless, let every one of you in particular so love his wife even as himself; and the wife see that she reverence her husband (Ephesians 5:33).**

I was watching a well-known couple on one of their teaching tapes. The wife was teaching, and I really admire her. She represents her well-known husband very well; her entire presentation was with sovereignty to her husband and office once she was through ministering. This really got to me, and I was humbled as I watched her walk over to her husband and hand him the microphone and kiss his hand, for him to immediately finish where she left off.

They were not competing with each other but completing the work of the Lord.

In the same spirit, he ushers in altar service with the anointing of God. The same couple has been an inspiration to me, as well as countless other couples. They clearly love and respect each other outwardly as well as behind closed doors. The pastor demonstrated one of my favorite scenes, which I personally like to do as well. The preacher held his wife in his arms as the spirit of God filled the room. It literally made me weep. If we can just continue to grow together, no weapon that's formed against us shall prosper.

"What then shall we say to these things? If God is for us, who can be against us?" (Romans 8:31, NKJV)

So, I salute those men of God everywhere that allowed God to make them men that revere their wife. I don't know how long it may have taken them to get to that place of reverence, but truly being that kind of example makes others want to live with the same kind of love and respect.

Shut Up & Go Through

Oftentimes in our lives, when we are faced with conflict, we tend to complain.

"We are troubled on every side, yet not distressed; we are perplexed, but not in despair" (2 Corinthians 4:8). About everything we were going through. Sometimes, we bring things on ourselves.

I remember in my early 20s, I dealt with a lot of past failures and regret. I was a junior mother in the church, a nurse, a choir director, an usher, and I watched over the young people for evening service; I was a young minister's wife, and I was potty training our oldest daughter. So not only was much given, much was required.

People expected a lot from me; my father (the pastor) wanted me to sit on the Mother's board, but my daughter was having accidents on my lap. So we went back and forth with me trying to be obedient and a mother. The other young people found fault with the way I carried myself. So my name was always in some sort of debate or conflict. I remember praying and telling God how overwhelmed I was about gossip and contempt. So, I prayed and told God

I hadn't done anything wrong to deserve being treated the way I was. Then God interrupted me and said, "My son didn't do anything either. But they lied on Him, mocked Him, whipped Him, and hung Him on the cross." That was my first awareness to "shut up and go through."

My second experience was when I had been married about five years and had two children, and we were having so many problems. He was working two jobs and in college; we were ships passing through the night. Looking and seeking relief, we decided to go to church that night. We went to a revival at the church we were visiting and later joined. The evangelist called my husband out, then asked, "Where is your wife?" The Lord really ministered to us through him. I felt compelled to talk to this minister about my marriage and problems. Surely, I thought, he was safe. Even then, God spoke, but I thought it was the devil intervening, so I could not get help. Not everyone is equipped to talk to you, especially in private. More secrets and shame that I had to confront and deal with. Throughout those dark, dreary days, I was going on a trip, explaining to one of my friends, Donna, what and how I felt, when this older mother in the church began to walk by my seat on her way to the front of the bus, and she leaned over and whispered in my ear and said, "God said, 'Shut up and go through.'" I immediately knew what God meant! Feeling ashamed, my friend asked, "What did she say?" I told her what she said, and she asked, "You took it?" I told her I knew what God meant because I failed to listen once again to His voice. I was tied to sin and his servant until I gave up everything, fully expecting to recover; I prepared myself for the worst. To my surprise, after much depression, God delivered me from me! Restored my marriage, and I love my husband more than ever. God can bring beauty out of ashes. Remember, watch as well as pray. My trust is only for God; man can disappoint you and have you question everyone in that office, literally. But God never fails; just go through it; somehow, He takes you through it all.

Spiritual Duty

"Wherefore be ye not unwise, but understanding what the will of the Lord *is*" (Ephesians 5:17). "There is a way which seemeth right unto a man, but the end thereof are the ways of death" (Proverbs 14:12).

Early when I married my husband, I admired his spiritual walk with the Lord; he was so anointed and sincere. I knew he loved the Lord with all his heart. Well, I felt that because I was a babe in the Lord, he was much more along than me. I proceeded to put him on a pedestal; I trusted him; he was my spiritual giant. But God came to me and gave me specific instructions to continue to cover him and have our marriage flow. I still remember my answer to God as though it were yesterday. The Lord instructed me to pray for my husband every day, interceding for him. My answer to the Lord God Almighty was no! Remember, I was only eighteen and crazy!

I proceeded to tell God that he didn't need any prayer; he's strong and spiritual. He should be praying for me so that I stay safe. He can pray for himself. After all, he's the preacher, not me! Well, I had it all wrong; a lot of my anger and resentment and pride came from being a preacher's daughter, having seen so much that it made me bitter. While I was learning to practice being submissive, I left God out. Thus, problems began to arise one after another. Being such a young wife, I was often misunderstood. I said to myself, I thought he loved me? How could he say these awful things to me? How could he go to sleep on me while I'm crying? How could the man that I felt so compatible with hurt me so bad? Well, God knew! And I didn't. Hell hath enlarged itself against us and our marriage and the future of our children. I had women tell me to my face, "How did you get him?" "He's fine, " and the list goes on. Some said they wanted him, and many sought for him to want them back.

"And Samuel said hath the Lord as *great* delight in burnt offerings and sacrifices, as in obeying the voice of the Lord? Behold, to obey is *better* than sacrifice, *and* to hearken than the fat of rams" (1 Samuel 15:22).

God had to restore our marriage. Hurt people end up hurting people. We had problems due to my disobedience; the enemy doesn't care that you both are chosen and your marriage is ordained by God; he just wants you to forget that.

"A little leaven leaveneth the whole lump" (Galatians 5:9).

We must learn to be obedient. Sometimes God will wake you up early at a certain time; you better get up and pray. Maybe He's told you too fast for your marriage or children. Your prayers could be turning the hands of death. We tend to ignore instructions when all is well. We only want to look at a map when we are lost. God wants us to keep in direct contact with Him. He's our compass.

"Thy word is a lamp unto my feet, and a light unto my path" (Psalm 119:105).

I paid a dear price for not heeding the voice of the Lord. Needless to say, the only giant in my life now is God.

But now, I pray for my husband all the time. Just before I began to write again this evening, he fell asleep with his head on my lap; the children were busy outside playing. So I began to whisper and pray and rub his head and ask God to continue to fill him with his spirit. He woke for a minute, looked into my eyes, and drifted back off to sleep. I used every moment to fortify his very being with prayer. It is our constant job. My reward is to see the peace of God in him. That's my joy.

Husbands should love their wives like Christ has loved the church. That's a huge job, and one most people really don't understand. But through the eyes of love and prayer, that pastor intercedes for his wife. Yes, lay those anointed hands on her sometimes; I am certain the Lord will show you really what His love is towards her.

Natural Duty

My girlfriend and I were talking about how my former pastor, at the time, had been out of town for two weeks, and his wife told the church he was now homesick and asked to give him a day to be with his wife and to get some rest. After church, some members came to the pastor's wife and said, "Are you serious? What are you going to do?" Now the preacher had not only missed being at church, but his natural duty to his home he missed. He wanted and needed the loving companionship of his wife, and she was more than willing to give it to him.

The church has to realize when not to bother the preacher. His wife has to squeeze in time to be with her husband a lot of times. She burns candles, makes special dinners, puts on her favorite lingerie. Only to find he's been retained by you. Many times, falling asleep hurts, sexually frustrated, and desperately wanting to fulfill all his desires; but she can only dream most of the time because he's so busy.

Just like the movie, many times, they push others to entertain their wives because of their schedule and need to please God; they forget their first ministry is their wife.

Even now, with all the administrative secretaries and executives this and that. They forget it's a job they are chosen for by God; they should not forget the other person in the office with them.

"Let the husband render with the wife due benevolence: and likewise also the wife unto the husband" (1 Corinthians 7:3).

The preacher's wife has to endure late-night counseling sessions, marital fights, clergy fights, laymen quarrels, meetings upon meetings. These days, the preacher's wife has to be mighty clever to spend quality time with her husband. She has to be creative and spontaneous, or she will feel neglected. I am reminded of a very sad story of a preacher's wife, one of many going through a painful divorce. The pastor, however, is accusing his wife of not being sexual enough toward him and other things she mentions to me.

Did he forget all the times he was on the phone for hours with other women while she waited in bed, and hours later, the kids would step over you, and you would sleep on the steps with the phone in your hand? That wife endured many years of sacrifice, but he remembers nothing. Please don't wait until it gets this far. Wives, sometimes you may have to go to his office with your fur coat or any coat on, lock the door. Have that lady at the front desk hold all calls and show up in your favorite suit! You are more than he could ever imagine! Afterward, unlock the door and leave.

You have the keys to this marriage. Plan getaways, leave special notes for him to meet you. Text him things he needs to hear from you. Why are we so shy about being his fantasy? Exceed his dream straight out of the park. Tell him what a great lover he is, even if he isn't, show him how to please you better. Cover all the bases, and there will be no room for the enemy.

You wear the brother out. Send him flowers or balloons. Stop waiting for him to dream up something special. If nobody ever taught him, he's not going to know how to plan and be your honored guest.

Do something special every month for just the two of you. Never be predictable; my husband doesn't know what I'm going to do next. I love to surprise him. If he wants something, I make it happen. My reward is what he gives me in return; it satisfies me. Kill every other desire for anything else. I hear some of you saying, I did that and more, and I still lost my husband! You are not the one at fault. God will judge him for his every action. I pray for the healing virtue of God over your life, and God can make up to you what the locust and the palmer worms have eaten! Your future will be greater than your past!

Finding Your Place

"He that dwelleth in the secret place of the Most High shall abide under the shadow of the Almighty" (Psalm 91:1).

As I spoke in earlier chapters, learning who you are is crucial. As a wife, mother, and spiritual leader, you have to constantly make time for yourself and your Master. It is through this time of intimacy that His image for your life is revealed. You will have many things in life you won't understand, but you must trust His plan for your life. I was always the one to try to analyze everything. As a child, I would hear the saints sing songs, and I would go home and ask my mother what they meant, and she would explain it to me. Well, as I got older, I became more curious. It was as if I had no fear; having survived sexual molestation in the family and out made me very suspicious of people. Around the time I got married, I somehow thought his love for me would erase all my pain. In my youthful thinking, I thought he could do what only Jesus could do. I later realized I needed prayer. Then I found out he had flaws in his character. After all, we were only human. I began to weep a lot and talk to God about him, mostly complaining over and over how "it isn't fair the way he treats me! God, you need to talk to him, make him change!" God would let me rumble and ramble, then ask me what was wrong with me. Many times, I would leave my prayer closet, wherever I was at that time, like, "God is a male chauvinist!" As I got older, our children had seen and heard so much arguing that they were confused. I really don't remember a lot of their growth. I was growing and having temper tantrums. I had not allowed God to grow in me. Finally, I started listening to God and allowing him to teach me, regardless of my marriage and family, God still wanted to be first in my life.

It really wasn't until after my mother died that I realized: what will my children think of me? What legacy of Christ in my life will I leave for them? Then God began to speak, and I listened because I was so broken. I've learned to forgive myself and love who I see in the mirror every day. Even with bodyweight issues and all, I'm learning that I must remember I'm his temple.

So, I desire to bring my life under the authority of Jesus Christ. As a pastor's wife, you must find your place. It may not be in the pulpit or sitting right beside him publicly. But one thing is for sure: your place is to make sure he knows he's loved and adored and feels safe in your arms.

I was reminded of a pastor that told me, after listening to me compliment my husband, that he wished his wife would touch him and admire him on how he dresses and takes care of himself. Basically, he was starving! And had I been the wrong type of woman, I could have soothed him and turned his passions toward me. We should never let our men crave for anything we know we can give them. He needs your heart, not humiliation or retaliation! We have an awesome role.

Some might say, "But you don't know my husband." That's true, but one thing for sure is that when you're walking in the spirit, atmospheres are supposed to change as you walk into a room! Don't settle for Satan's packages when God has given us power in the natural and spiritual realm to fight any force against us. Blow his mind and perhaps yours too. You are fearfully and wonderfully made. You are His design; He did not make a mistake!

God has not and will not forget you!

Abandoned

What happens when the preacher's wife goes through raising children by herself? Even when two people made the child, or perhaps the couple goes through a divorce? Or the other spouse dies? They have to bear the children, sometimes with a heavy heart.

If your husband is full-time in the ministry, most of the time, he's so busy mending everybody else's wounds he forgets his own wife.

You have pastors caught in infidelity that have fathered outside children. And that wife has to endure that shame and humiliation not only to their children but to the congregation. Many times they divorce, and the pastors commit suicide! What shame to live with, yet raising your children. How do you get past that? Nobody but God could. The children would need special trips and quiet time, with simple hugs and kisses to feel loved. In most cases, the mother has to try and fulfill both roles. In a divorce, the child goes through a lot of emotional trauma, identity issues. "Who am I? Why weren't we enough? Why did dad leave us?"

The wife often blames herself, being so stressed out

when her husband leaves her for another woman…or even another man! That wife will feel less than a woman, with all kinds of frustrations which alter her ability to function as a mother. The rejection that woman feels is indescribable. Only God can heal that broken heart.

In most cases, more than likely, the children will blame the mother for not being enough for daddy, especially if he takes his life.

When, in fact, daddy is the one with the problem. Hence, the mother not only has to deal with her deep-seated emotion but her children as well.

How can you bring balance to your child's life when yours is waiting in the balance? God can heal the hurt. If walls haven't been built up so high, no one can come in and hurt them again. With all the hurt the wife suffers from, she too will find it hard to talk with anyone about her home. There is no safe place.

"He that abideth in the secret place of the most High, shall abide under the shadow of the Almighty" (Psalm 91:1).

So many people will spread your business, but God will give you somebody that will pray, and talk with you, and even weep with you until you feel your heart mending and all those broken pieces coming back together again. So you can be whole and complete naturally, as well as spiritually.

Also, during those times, women attack themselves, their bodies, and personality, but you need to look in the mirror and find at least one thing you know looks good and say every day, "God made me this way, and I'm beautiful!" Say it until you believe it! Love yourself, and you will feel better about yourself, and better will come. Some women get cosmetic work done; that's a matter of choice, but do what makes you feel like a million dollars.

Forgive Then Forget

Forgiving is easier said than done, that is what most people will tell you, but I won't because I've had to learn how to, on countless occasions. And just when I thought it was over, it came up again like vomit.

Since I was a little girl, it seemed like forgiveness was expected of me naturally. Having come through being molested and raped by members inside and outside the family, I had to learn to forgive. However, deep inside, I was ashamed, bitter, and I blamed myself. I learned to live with secrets. So, when I got married at eighteen years old, I thought, surely my life could stop going up and down. Because I loved him so much, nothing could be that bad. To my naïve surprise, we hadn't experienced anything yet.

So, first came words, said in anger or ignorance, we couldn't take back. Resentment started growing. Angrily thinking, I would say to myself I was just fine by myself. Naturally and literally speaking, in our earlier days of marriage, we verbally offended each other a lot. So, every time we had a discussion, we brought up what happened in the last disagreement. We really didn't know how to forgive, then forget. Over twenty-plus years ago, in the church, no

43

one we knew was teaching marriage survival.

There were times when the enemy would send different people in your life to make you think, *Wow, I married the wrong person!* A lot of relationships were not sexual, even though that was the plan. Mainly, it caused division in the home. We really didn't fully understand why. We were left with unanswered questions. So, you begin to blame yourself, looking in the mirror, *What does she/he have that I don't?* During those times, God isn't sought after at all. Because you're hurt and operating in the flesh, seeking to feel better. One thing we figured out was hurt people, hurt people.

A whole lot of couples in the church needed counseling before marriage—like we did!—but didn't know who to go to. One thing my husband and I have always done was be honest with each other. If I came to him with an issue, he let me know if it was true or false. I would do the same. Now, the truth isn't always pretty, but after over thirty-plus years of marriage, the truth stands on its own. We had to learn to forgive and forget. Because if you keep remembering, then you will be looking back in torment! The enemy will give you an excuse to do it. We've seen many couples divorce—ever since we've been married, mostly—because of adultery, money, and pride! I have wept over many failed marriages. Many thought they needed an exit. Forgiveness is not a choice; you must do it! If you want to see God in peace. Even if you feel your marriage is over, God gives you an exit (adultery) if you can't forget. He knew some people would not be able to go on. But His grace is sufficient, wherever you need Him to be.

Because I've experienced so much in my marriage, I don't play with the devil anymore. Be it male/female, you will get checked! I'm not a babe in Christ anymore. I know that spirit of lust and perversion when I see it. You have to let that spirit know and expose it. It's just a familiar spirit with a different name and face. Learn to say, "No more, " forever in Jesus' name! Now, you can't make anyone stay married to you that wants to leave. Let them go! It's their loss. God will make it up to you. Don't beg, get your cry on and pull yourself together.

You might be larger in size than you were, your hair might be falling out; get a weave! Loose teeth? Go to the dentist. Go to the gym. But whatever you do, be a lady! I once had a friend that was always beautiful and curvaceous. One day her husband came home and said, "I don't love you anymore. I'm leaving." She was devastated! I remember her saying when they met with the pastor to try and get help that he said more hurtful things. She said she wanted to stab him with a fork. But he still would have left her, fork in him and all. Still, she ached for him because she was still in love with him. But they divorced. And some years later, she married again and even had a child when the doctors said no!

God made it up to her because she was willing to forgive and forget.

Another couple: a young minister got married to this gorgeous young woman, and after only a couple months of marriage, he left and moved out, declaring that he tried all he knew how and he was tired. Meanwhile, he left his wife two months pregnant, without a job or income; and he left with another man! He was gay, and he even denied the baby.

But the child came out looking just like him. That young minister's wife went through all types of pain and rejection! But forgiveness was possible. That young woman had to forgive and forget, so her child could have a relationship with her father. He is still in the closet. That woman is successful now, ministering to others in pain, and because of her great strength and character, God blessed her with another minister and has given her double for her shame. Forgiveness is powerful! She now has the marriage of her dreams; they really love each other. I call them the dream team!

I knew of another preacher's wife; her husband said he was going through a midlife crisis. He didn't want his wife anymore after ten-plus years of marriage. She always showed him so much public affection, but he literally put her out! This was long before Tyler Perry's movie. He, too, moved his younger woman into their home. She cried and cried daily and talked about him openly due to her pain. Finally, I told her, "If you want your husband back, shut up and take him back!" It's not our business. She was even suicidal because of the public shame. He also had a child with the other woman and everything. So she forgave him, and we all shut up too. And we treated him like he never left. Now, that's learned behavior and love. To keep showing the love of Christ. I've seen a lot and experienced it too. So, therefore, we are living proof you can forgive and forget.

"Brethren, I count not myself to have apprehended: but this *one* thing *I do,* forgetting those things which are behind, and reaching forth unto those things which are

before" (Philippians 3:13).

There was another preacher's wife that I will refer to as Ethel I met. She was a wonderful human being, sweet, kind, and Holy Ghost filled when she became a wife. Ethel met and married what appeared to be a godly preacher, who said he was totally smitten by her and that, according to his prayer list, she was the perfect wife for him. She met all the checks and balances.

They had a beautiful wedding and, shortly after, she became pregnant even though she was on the pill. She was taken by surprise but happy. However, her husband was sad, became verbally abusive and upset.

He said he only wanted her, no children yet! They both had good jobs and credit until the wife got laid off. She never really had to depend on a man or anyone because she always worked. He made her feel useless; she had delivered their son, and, shortly after, she conceived again.

Yes, she was fertile! Her husband resented the children, so she had suffered him being nasty and abusive; never home, he was working, in school, and detached. When she asked to talk, he would yell and scream and even got physically abusive towards her and their children. Fear was running that home. All in all, they shared three children, and

48

she did get back on her feet righteously! They purchased a home, and the children were growing and excelling in school.

But when she went to work and the father was at home with the children, it should have been downtime, but he wanted quiet, so he would yell and literally fight the children.

"Fathers, provoke not your children to *anger*, lest they be discouraged" (Colossians 3:21).

In their home, he didn't want to make repairs; the wife's hands were tied. Her husband was making a six-figure income, yet he was not taking care of taxes properly for the IRS. The wife began to get notices of things she thought were taken care of already, credit card bills, mortgage payments late, student loan payments, etc.

This couple was living in anger and torment. The church thought he was too perfect for any correction; after all, he was very smart and intelligent, and it must have been that wife. He made her whole demeanor change. Ultimately, a big fight erupted. He later left... It's been years now.

He has chosen to be homeless; even now, he has a new woman. All his children are grown and doing very well, under the circumstances of living with constant turmoil. His once A+ credit is gone, and all his creditors have contacted his wife. The IRS wanted to seize the property too.

After over twenty-plus years of marriage and almost five years of separation, they are getting a divorce. He filed. She even asked him to come back home several times, but what's so remarkable now is Ethel said God told her to forgive him totally and that He would bless her!

She said, "Debra, I let go and forgave him." She said, "Wow, now God is opening doors." She said the house had been re-done from the roof to the back door. Now all her desires are being met, the blessings of the Lord are overtaking her. Now she is waiting for the judge to sign the decree of divorce. Ethel said her former husband looks bad, and now the other woman is calling her to ask if he has mental problems.

I told her to say a few things to the other woman, but she said, "No, God told me to let it go, forgive and move on!" Her testimony really blessed me because I know how she cried and struggled and asked God what was wrong with her. The rejection a woman feels when her husband desires everyone else but his wife and family. He rarely went to school events, doctor visits, or planned family trips, or just enjoyed his life. He lost his six-figure job during a difficult time in his life because he didn't listen to his wife on how to protect his job.

Now he calls her, asking to borrow money. It's insane how he had it all but despised his life because it wasn't how he planned it. I am godly proud of this woman of God for forgiving him. Now she is resting in the obedience of God. Stop fighting with the situation, and the battle is not yours but the Lord's. Let Him take over and silence the haters. Forgive your enemies, then ask God to help you to forget the hurt and the shame. She is proof He will do just what He said if we just trust and believe His word.

Dangers of Strife

The day I realized I had it, the Lord broke me all the way down; I couldn't wait until my husband returned to tell him he was right! All those times he told me I had it, I thought he was trying to hurt me or insult me. I was too submissive to have strife! Oh, I was wrong. Somewhere in my heart, I never let go of past failures in our marriage with our children and other relationships. I was ruled by the pain of the past. And whenever I hurdled, I reminded him. When he would tell me God could not bless the ministry until that spirit was dealt with, I would be so hurt because everything was personal to me, and what a burden that if the ministry failed, it would be my fault. I never asked for the ministry, and now if it fails, it's going to be my fault. The enemy does not care how he comes to divide and steal.

"The thief cometh not, but for to steal, and kill, and to destroy: I am come that they might have life, and that they might have *it* more abundantly" (John 10:10).

Just as long as he's invited in, not only will he steal, but kill and destroy. While we're busy rehashing the past, with familiar spirits, our children and church family feel the emotions of a topsy-turvy home. They hear the screams, see the tears, feel the sound of doors slamming and remember only what they have heard and seen. Comforting them comes Satan's voice, the accuser of the brethren. He immediately tells the children mommy and daddy hate each other, and they're going to kill each other. They're going to get a divorce; which one do you want to live with? Many times we apologize to our mates and go on, but never to our children for what they have heard and seen but don't understand. I've always explained our behavior to our children, good or bad. Because I didn't want them to think what we were portraying was acceptable behavior to God. Now, you might say my husband thinks he's never wrong. That's okay. We got a formula for that. Do not try to wrestle with the flesh.

"For we wrestle not against flesh and blood, but against principalities, against powers, against rulers of darkness of this world, against spiritual wickedness in high *places*" (Ephesians 6:12).

Because that's one of the definitions of strife. We're going to take the relationships to God in prayer. You might say, "Not me, Lord, but him! Lord help us." For we are no longer two but one. Our prayer life is personal; it's one of the biggest tricks of Satan to make it personal, and you get pitiful and distraught. It's time to tell Satan, looking down at him, "This home belongs to the Lord! This relationship belongs to God." Anoint every doorpost, walk and pray around the house; anoint his shoes so that he would walk and be guided by God. Anoint him while he's sleeping, when he's in the shower; anoint the clothes he's preparing to put on the children because we've allowed that spirit to roam. Take authority and dominion back over yourself and your home. That spirit leaves you, but many times, not your home. You wonder why you're struggling with the children: we gave that spirit dominion in our home. Now go and take it back.

I will never forget some years ago, my husband and I were having an argument and came upstairs to go to our bedroom, and my oldest daughter, Ericka, said she saw an evil spirit also walking behind my husband as we entered our bedroom. We stopped a lot after that! We've been given an awesome responsibility in the home, working outside or not. Our homes are what make them, no excuses. Please take a stroll through your home and see if you like what you've made. That was in the natural world; now, do a spiritual walk and label what you see if you have more evil than good residing in your home. You just might have been invaded by the enemy. He now comes through television, cable, and even cartoons, games, and all forms of witch-craft; computers, all kinds of devices. Yet we are sleeping. The enemy really doesn't have to knock your door down to get in…he has the front door key!

So, now you have to go into the enemy's camp and get your home, your children, your marriage, and take back what he has stolen from you! No matter how you look at it, he's a thief! Once you take back your territory, God can come and heal, repair and give us His righteousness again in the home.

We've operated so long without it; we don't recognize the word. What if my husband won't pray with me? Then, you pray; perhaps we've caused so much damage with our mouth and ways, he's turned off.

So, pray until God deals with his heart, pray until he feels safe in his own home! Pray until peace hits him at the door. Keep praying until the demons tremble!

Pray over the witchcraft and rebellious spirits of your children. Honey, after a while, he'll be leading the prayer because, after all, you can't act like you're having too much excitement without him being the head; he will find his way back to the body.

Ladies, it will be worth it all when you allow God to free you. I was so relieved. I don't want to lose my deliverance to anyone. I'm very careful. When those old thoughts arrive at my spirit door, I proclaim whom the Son sets free is free indeed.

After years of strife, I want to be able to look at my husband and just love him. The rest is God's job and was never mine from the beginning. Honor your marriage vows, do not substitute them; you can not alter God's words. Only obey and adhere to them. Love, as God has loved us. This book is to give knowledge and wisdom and insight. Not to start bickering, but to challenge you to know God, and He will teach you to know the preacher so you can be the *real* preacher's wife.

Pacifiers versus Passersby

Now, in the late '90s, I saw positive role models that gave their wives due benevolence. Because of that, I can't honor them enough. It's a real man that realizes that he married the queen of his heart. These days, my husband and I have worshipped at another ministry, and for the past three years, every time, without fail, when he stands before the congregation, he honors his wife as the only lady for him! I love it.

It's a powerful declaration; whether they receive it or not, he has set the atmosphere to honor his beloved. So, I exhort you, men of God, to continue to love and cherish her continually like a circle of love.

But there are some preacher's wives that abuse their position, for whatever reason, and their husbands pacify their every whim even if it hurts the body of Christ.

I remember one incident when I called the preacher's home. Now, my mother always taught me to greet the wife first, then ask for the pastor, and I did. But when she said hello… The people at the sports bar were kinder than she.

I introduced myself to her, and she calmed down and proceeded to give the phone to her husband. But what if I had been a member of the church, perhaps considering suicide, some type of trauma, anything? I probably would have taken my life if I were that member. That preacher's wife was rude, obnoxious, and from what I hear: she bosses him around in that church some terribly; hence, creating an atmosphere of no respect with their many children and at that ministry. Wives, we can make or break a ministry; being foolish has death-related consequences and helps no one.

"Forsake the foolish, and live; and go in the way of understanding. A foolish woman is clamorous: she *is* simple, and knoweth nothing" (Proverbs 9:6, 13).

You also have some wives that accuse everybody of wanting their husband. We can only speculate how they get there. I've always said that if a woman is jealous, more than likely someone gave her a reason, but some are for no reason at all. They kill the church; the members have no confidence in their leader because he really isn't allowed to be a leader.

"For if a man know not how to rule his own house,

**how shall he take care of the church of God?"
(1 Timothy 3:5)**

**"Husbands, love your wives, even as Christ also loved the church and gave himself for it"
(Ephesians 5:25).**

Passersby are preachers that obviously have their heads in the clouds. You just can't continue to ignore your greatest supporter; she's the mother of your children if you're blessed to have any. She's the accountant, she's the cook, the designer, the seamstress, your therapist, she's your lover, and the list can go on and on. In the church, she's the secretary, the choir president, the women's board, cleaning committee, pastor's aide, and amen corner; she's your best advertisement. Continue to allow your wife to be proud to be called more than just a preacher's wife but your wife. Nothing and nobody should look better than her, smell better, or talk better in your eyes! There will always be someone better, but no one should be bigger than her in your life.

I always tell or compliment my husband on how cute and handsome he is. And now that we are older and all the kids are gone, his grey hair is amazing on him. I tell him he looks good, and he does! Nobody can capture my spirit and soul like my husband because that's who I love, and incidentally, he has been an incredible man of God and example in our home. There have been advances made towards me as well, but my role is to be faithful to God, and by default, I will be faithful to my husband.

The Protector

It's a wonder the preacher's wife has any self-esteem. Constantly, people come and lash at her for one reason or another. But I think the most common is people within the church that really don't want to see a positive relationship between the preacher and his wife. They automatically think of ways to turn them against each other. Of course, it's a trick from the enemy, but it happens. The most common question is: "How did you get a pastor?" Or "I wish I could find somebody just like him, " or "I need to talk to the pastor in private."

She constantly receives ridicule and shame; the enemy usually comes in more times than we care to mention. Yes, preachers can succumb to these advances too.

"For we all have sinned, and come short of the glory of God" (Romans 3:23).

Some have come up and said, "Your husband sure looks good, " "Your husband sure smells good, " etc. Mind you, some of these women are single, but most are married and forgot! They are so busy trying to water someone else's grass that when theirs is dead, it's only because they let it die.

The preacher's wife gets lustful advances made towards her as well. But by far, the women supersede the men. As I have watched over the years, there are certain things another woman is not supposed to have access to your husband without your consent. Preparing his lunches and bringing them to the church; especially preparing cakes that the wife is not allowed to even sample (we know why). Special luncheons and banquets he's invited to, but not his wife. Doing his laundry—all the jobs that belong to his wife. Wives, don't give away your authority, either.

"Every wise woman buildeth her house: but the foolish plucketh it down with her hands" (Proverbs 14:1).

Our husbands are to provide for us, and we need to be their protectors. We are to pray for them and shield them from Temptress Suzy and Tempting Tom, even when he believes she is humble and he is being just kind.

The preacher's wife's role never ends. I'm reminded of a very well-known couple in the clergy that failed, and it was public many years ago.

I was really not that concerned about him, even though I prayed for him. It was his wife that my heart went out to. Even in pain, we still have to be wives; even with unanswered questions, we have to up gird and warfare with them in prayer. Behind closed doors, I know she agonizes over the situation, being blamed for not taking care of her husband's sexual desires. For all we know, she did.

"But every man is tempted, when he is drawn away of his own lust and enticed. Then when lust hath conceived, it bringeth forth sin: and sin, when it is finished, bringeth forth death" (James 1:14-15).

Oftentimes, the preacher's wife doesn't have the luxury of being in pain and having someone tell her, "It's going to be alright." Many times, hearing "I love you" and "I'm sorry" becomes limited because she has to mend the wounds of the preacher, going into severe depression and thoughts of suicide; she spends so much time pulling and praying him out of his situation that her hurt gets pushed into the lower level of her heart.

After many countless days and months of turmoil, they bounce back, and the preacher's wife is still there wondering, *When will it be my turn for healing?* She yet has to endure shame and often public humiliation. I saw a recent picture or interview of a couple and their multimillion-dollar church and school empty, their dream all dried up. All I saw was how much she had aged. Yet, the pastor still seems arrogant.

She still was his shield of protection, even when she tried to be his closest friend. He doesn't seek her; it's someone else.

Wisdom Builds a Home

"Who can find a virtuous woman? for her price is far above rubies. The heart of her husband doth safely trust in her, so that he shall have no need of spoil" (Proverbs 31:10, 11).

This book has been a journey of my life, throughout now almost thirty-nine years of marriage to one man! God has been faithful to us. I had to learn how to be a wife at the young age of eighteen. A lot of times, I was foolish with the words of my mouth. I'm very impulsive, so there were times I would speak first and think later.

My husband was from a large family; his parents separated when he was young. He suffered from low self-esteem. He had six brothers; all of them, including him, were good-looking men, but they were missing being fathered. We knew very little about being married, except for the fact that God ordained it. The church, however, kept telling us it was better to marry than burn. Guess we were all burning, so we both came out with character issues.

Even though my parents were still married, they weren't as happy as I expected them to be. I thought to myself, *I will show them all how to be happily married.*

We experienced financial problems, and I wanted him to make them go away like a real man would. But I was not using wisdom, so we would get vexed and not talk to each other for days. Then we would communicate, repent and try all over again, God's way.

But I began to withhold my feelings and not say how I felt, and still, it came out through my actions. I couldn't hide what was going on inside. I began to get angry and bitter, thinking that after all, I could have stayed single and done badly by myself. Now we both have one another's luggage, and it wasn't designer luggage either!

So, I began to ask God for the spirit of longsuffering. Now, you know I was confused, that's something you don't have to ask for; it comes with the package. My love for God made me seek out wisdom. I did not want to be a silly woman. Feeling isolated, you can't share your personal life with others. God was the one I vented to. It was not a lot of teaching in the church back then, just hardcore COGIC, but that's all they knew.

One thing I'm forever grateful for is the foundation: my mother taught us to pray and recognize demon spirits. Even in me. So I had to learn to speak the scriptures over our lives and pray. Because we can build our home with our hands, and with those same hands tear it and the church down. Many times as the pastor's wife, you can see the devils when they walk into the church. If you're governed by wisdom, you can't go right up to them and expose Satan. But the power of God in you can change the very atmosphere to allow them to know you will stay and be free, or you can flee.

No one is playing with that spirit anymore. Now, your mate may not see what you have seen, and you can't beat him up for it. But you can ask God to sharpen his discernment, to open his eyes and ears for the kingdom. Because the moment you jump, defensive, they become the shepherd, not your husband, lover, and friend, and they want to protect the sheep, not you! So, wisdom, my dear sister says, "let patience have her perfect work." Sit back, be beautiful and watch and pray. Then, when he comes home with something to tell you, burning in his heart, be attentive and listen; then, if he's really a man after God's heart, he will admit it. I know God showed you, and I didn't want to see it, and finally, wisdom won. Not people: God will teach him to work with your gift, not against it. You don't want to be accused of hindering the ministry's growth with jealousy and everything that Satan brings. Acting foolishly allows your mate to see Jesus in you. Then and only then will he respect the anointing that rests in your life.

I once talked to another friend about her backsliding husband who was smoking and drinking and cursing. She said she hated it. And was concerned about him drinking and driving. So, I said, when he's at home, wisdom says to love him straight out of sin. Prop his legs up, hand him his beer, and constantly pray for him. He's still your husband; honor him so he can see Jesus, not you. It's been a while now, and that husband delivered, preaching the gospel! They built a new home, and he fully furnished it. Before the house was built, I told her to fortify that home with prayer and thanksgiving. God was faithful to His word.

I just heard a story of another preacher's wife that got up to have words at their church appreciation regarding her husband. She politely said in her testimony, "I thank God for my husband, my friend, my lover, and to Sister Chewing Gum, his lover too!" Needless to say, the church went into an uproar. Now, she may have had a right to confront him privately, but not publicly. She was led by her pain and became foolish, not using wisdom, considering the souls that could be lost.

When Witchcraft Visits the Pulpit

It comes in many different forms, but the one I would like to bring to focus is when man meets beast. So often, the beast is another woman/man. Now, it doesn't necessarily mean she/he looks like a beast. But they entrap their prey as one. Many times, the preacher's wife can see her/him for what they are. But the man of God is temporarily blinded, just long enough so the temptress/tempter can work their powers. Now, you might say, "How can this be?" They easily take their eyes off God. You may feel, *Isn't the preacher spiritual and knows all?* Yes and no.

He may be spiritual but does not know it all. Oftentimes, they are so sweet and cunning and attentive to the pastor that he puts his guard down. Pushing away guidelines from the Holy Spirit and warnings from his wife. Replacing all of his instinct, which cannot be seen with what he naturally sees. And before you know it, he's not the same man you married. He's never at home, his attention is being given to the other woman. His time is unaccountable for; not even cheap pagers, people have cell phones everywhere now, even on their wrists. His personality type is always tense, very irritable; every little word mentioned is nagging and argumentative so he can leave. About this time, he knows but doesn't know how to get out of it. He just knows he can not be in your presence.

The preacher's wife has to pray and fast that God would lose the hold that the enemy has on his mind. It all starts in the mind.

I was reminded of an incident where not only did that spirit want the head of the house, but didn't stop until it slept with the pastor's whole house. Not only was that spirit not denounced, but it has been allowed to stay! The devil is a lie! You have got to go!

"O foolish Galatians, who hath bewitched you? That ye should not obey the truth..." (Galatians 3:1).

"Casting down imaginations, and every high thing that exalteth itself against the knowledge of God, and bringing into captivity every thought to the obedience of Christ" (2 Corinthians 10:5).

I personally know of so many clergies that have fallen prey to this spirit and refuse to deal with it. Because the sin feels good to them; their mind is seared with a hot iron.

Some have said, "that's between me and God." Some preachers' wives have also fallen prey to this spirit because the strong man got bind first, then it was easy to take his house! As women, we have to declare war on the enemy! Even if it means we lose our spouse. Plead the blood of Jesus every day; decree and declare that Satan will not have your husband, your children, or your ministry. Fight in the spirit, not in the flesh. Anoint all his clothes and shoes, where he lay in the bed; everything in his office at the church, his car, everything! If you feel like a fool, it will be for Christ's sake.

I have watched God turn marriages around. The wife sometimes had to go get the husband out of the brothel, etc. But don't give the enemy your marriage on a silver platter. He is yet the righteous seed. The battle is not yours but the Lord's; He will give you release as to when to stop praying.

Unfortunately, the church suffers from the influence of demons. I suggest, if you sense this spirit in your leaders, pray for them and ask God to reveal to them the body of Christ, and leave! Your family legacy depends on it. Spirits will attach themselves to your home, and you will ponder, *Where did that come from? I didn't want to do that or this?* If he can no longer watch for your soul, then you must leave and ask God for another leader.

Godly Discipline

"Fathers, provoke not your children to anger, lest they be discouraged" (Colossians 3:21).

Sometimes, we cause wrath in our homes when we have issues we haven't dealt with. The children are often the ones we practice our frustration on. One thing I found to be true is people will pressure you on how to raise your children when they don't do a good job on their own. Growing up as a preacher's child, people would always say—mind you, mostly saints— "The preacher's kids are the worst kids, you know!" Well, we weren't! But those were the voices allowed to speak in our atmosphere and belittle our parents. No one should have that much control, verbally abusing your seed. In fact, if they are not speaking life, they definitely should not be allowed to speak death!

"Death and life *are* in the power of the tongue [...]" (Proverbs 18:21).

If, by chance, your children were actively working in the church, then you were persecuted as being the only ones that could do anything in ministry. Basically, the naysayers could not be pleased. That's why, when I began to have children, I accepted advice, but God was the head in our home. Unlike my parents, our neighbors couldn't discipline our children; unless we really knew them, they could tell our children right from wrong. But we didn't allow anyone to brand them so they could feel better or worse. When our children were small, I really never had to discipline our oldest. It was always our son throughout school. If I had allowed people to guide me and not God, we would have ruined our children. I remember when a couple of the children would wet the bed. People told me to beat their behinds, and they wouldn't wet the bed anymore. I didn't feel led to do that. I provided clean sheets and a spray bottle for them to clean and change their beds and assured them in love they would grow out of it, and they did! A couple of times, they were away from home and had an accident and got beat. So, they didn't go back over there. God gives us clear guidelines on how to raise our children correctly. We must follow his plan to receive his promise.

I remember, as the children got to their teen years, I tried to tame my oldest son. I went to his room with my belt. Of course, he wouldn't bend over, so when I attempted to swing, he took the belt from me. I was so ashamed all we could do was laugh. He said, "Mama, I'm too big for this." So I had to figure something else out.

We talked to my oldest daughter Ericka, who always got in trouble for talking too much; she always wanted to have the last word! Deidra, the baby, was all of them in one. Correcting her was a chore, but we had to. The younger brothers we adopted were constantly fighting over one thing or another. We really battled with rebellious spirits and generational curses from their birth families. Having been raised in the system, with no guidelines, our home was too structured and disciplined for them. We had to change the way they thought. "Call the police on us; we are your legal parents now." They brought a whole new world to our home. The police were always there; they were runaways and could not accept discipline. It was very tough. They had no godly fear or reverence. We had to teach them the word of the Lord. They did not understand honoring your parents so that your days may be long on earth. They could care less. We began to let them read the word as punishment, even though they still said they didn't understand. I can firmly say: don't let rebellion into your home on any scale. It's witchcraft and control, and, sooner or later, it will manifest itself.

We literally had fights with those boys; they were kicked out of local stores for theft, schools, therapists, etc. I had no idea my passion to adopt would be more than we could handle! Countless hospital visits to get them back med compliant.

Anger beyond anything we saw with our birth children. Until finally, my husband said, after a fistfight and almost drug overdose of our son, that he couldn't come back. He was twenty years old at the time, and the youngest got kicked out of a wonderful school because he wanted to sell drugs. So, ultimately, he also moved out and ran away before his eighteenth birthday. We knew we had done everything spiritually and naturally that we could for them to feel safe and secure.

The youngest is in and out of correctional facilities, and the oldest one we talk to all the time. He is in a group home. Mentally, they will always need some form of assistance. But they are still our children, yet to battle for their soul. If you are battling anything with your children, don't blame each other because you are going to have to be a team to get through this. Whatever God gives you to do for your family, complete it. Be a doer of His word, not just a hearer. I pray for your strength and endurance in Christ Jesus and His anointing on the presence of flesh. We almost became prisoners in the house, we could go nowhere, nobody wanted to watch them. I even wondered why we did what we did, adopting them.

Make time for each other!

Now our house is empty. Deidra just got married. And it's our time now, after thirty-nine years of marriage; it's back to where it all started: just us. And we love it!

Till Death Do Us Part

"Nevertheless let every one of you in particular so love his wife even as himself; and the wife see that she reverences her husband" (Ephesians 5:33).

As I pen this book, I hope it has been a help to the ministry. If your marriage is whole and complete: pray for other marriages. If your husband has fallen from grace: pray that God will reconcile him to Christ. When he has been embraced with Christ, then God can put your marriage back together again. So, if you're contemplating marriage, pray for a man of the Bible, what God describes as a man. Pray that God will allow him to love and lead you like Christ loved the church.

My next story came to me a few years ago; it shook me very hard, I became overwhelmed and angry at God. This couple, who will remain anonymous, was married for over thirty-plus years. They had several grown children; they had been in pastoral ministry and were very committed. The preacher's wife was the gentlest woman you would ever want to meet. She was clean, honest, hospitable, friendly, and she knew how to reach God; she had an awesome prayer life.

She taught women, her home life was not perfect, nor her health, but you would have never known it looking at her. She battled many issues.

The pastor, her husband, had not always been spiritually sound, nor was his behavior. Many times, he brought her embarrassment; oftentimes, too much to bear. But she continually sought hard after God. Her children knew she loved God because she showed them, even when their father forgot he was a preacher. She held that family together like glue; even through secret illness, she taught by precept and example. I'm leaving out many distasteful things in this story, but will share what I'm allowed.

"Husbands, love your wives, even as Christ also loved the church and gave himself for it" (Ephesians 5:25).

Marriage vows were broken in the worst way. As a younger preacher's wife, I watched down through the years how the woman made sacrifices without even putting their careers on hold for the family. Was it worth it? Well, the wife, after many years of taking care of everyone but herself, became very ill. First, high blood pressure crept in, then diabetes and insulin dependence, which drained her daily; yet, she was still pushed to complete all her church duties. Then, finally, cancer struck her body, and within six months, she was gone. That's not the ugly part of the story either; during her sickness, when she needed her husband the most, the husband could not handle her sickness, and it seemed he wanted her to die. She was hospitalized off and on. So she instructed one of her children to buy their father a pager so he would be reachable at all times, in case anything happened.

After staring death in the face, she also faced betrayal from her husband, who sought solace in the arms of another woman (the beast).

The children took shifts to take care of their mom while fighting with their father on the other hand. This woman loved this man so much that she gave her whole life for him and her children, but he couldn't hold her hand as she stood at death's door. I know now she was in deep pain, scared, lonely, and yet continuing to have faith in God for healing. She could barely breathe; she couldn't sleep because of constant coughing. The husband took the cowardly approach and would not stay. If she got out of her hospital bed to lay next to him, he would get up and comment, "I don't want to be sick too, " and he would leave! She wasn't sick, she was dying! She wanted nothing but his comfort for all those years of being his church, when he didn't have any members yet, raising his children, while he was busy working, taking care of that household. Being his friend, his mother, his lover, his everything. Yet he couldn't comfort her, even till her death. By the way, the other woman even made phone calls to this woman on her sickbed and told her, "I want your husband." He refused to talk or comfort her. But she knew her husband was operating under the influence of witchcraft and too arrogant to know.

She died in the Lord but unhappy, with a broken heart and many unanswered questions and regrets. It was too late. Besides God to trust in, she had her children to take care of her, which is whom she releases herself with. Shortly after the wife died, the preacher instructed the children to come and get their mother's clothing. Then, a couple of months following the death, he married another woman. I learned after this example and her experience that you should take care of yourself because you are replaceable! Even if that man was scared and didn't want to lose his wife, turning to witches and warlocks was not the solution.

He should have given her all the love and respect she had given him. And he will go to his grave not being able to fix what he messed up. I heard an old mother of eighty-three years say the other day, "Look really good at those seeds in your hand before you throw them out because you will reap what you sow." This man has suffered, but half of it has not been told yet. After all those years of being married, he hadn't discovered that love is not conditional—it's unconditional. God and time have healed the wounds that those children and grandchildren had to go through. But it also gave them a new awareness about life; their mother had always taught them lessons, even on her deathbed.

Take care of all your business, and especially your children, because when it's all said and done, you could be treated as nothing more than a bond servant's child. When this great woman died, she was remembered for being who she was. You see, that's something no one knows; that amount of distress and pain can be taken away from you. Even to this day, over a decade later, people still talk about the work she did. She left a legacy and her dignity.

"Wherefore they are no more twain, but one flesh. What therefore God hath joined together, let not man put asunder" (Matthew 19:6).

Fight for the Children

As I spoke of before, learn to live while you love and laugh. My husband is a licensed home contractor, so I have helped him with drywall, down to plumbing. It's amazing how much you can talk about doing projects together. It also eases a lot of stress. We have five children, two of which we adopted are biological brothers. All of our children now range from thirty-seven to twenty-six, and we have four granddaughters, three grandsons, and one on the way. So we spend a lot of time thinking about the children and helping out so that we literally have to make time to love and laugh.

Our oldest son has always been busy from the time he was a baby. He always wanted to be just like his dad. All during my pregnancy with all my children, I gave them back to God. I also asked God for special musical gifts in their lives. Well, E2—as he prefers to be called—started out with the drums at age two; Ericka, the oldest, was practicing playing the piano when E2 asked if he could play, and of course, she said no. They were eight and ten at the time. Somehow, he got on the keyboard and began to play everything he heard his sister play. Ericka got discouraged and stopped, and the rest is history. He sought to play everything he heard, and we began to shelter him from all types of people and spirits. Or so we thought. He began to play for our ministry when we started, and we all did worship together. He was very gifted and anointed for worship. Pastors everywhere wanted him to play. He was still in his early teens. The danger is you're not there, as he goes to these many places. During times of ups and downs of ministry, we neglected, unknown the other children in the house. Children get discouraged in ministry, too; as you are being obedient, leaving other ministries, the children are aching for the friends they left. Many times without saying goodbye. They resent you and your God. So we tend to nurse our wounds from discouragement and forget they got cut too. We let our spiritual antennas down. We feel that because your children are with Pastor so and so, they would look out for your child. Truth is that people look out for themselves! Our son basically left our ministry and moved out of the house at sixteen with another older musician because we were too strict. For a while, we didn't hear from him or see him.

Other church people told him we were trying to take his passion and gift from him. I ached for my son! I cried and was bitter towards everybody of influence in his life.

I didn't want to associate myself with anyone that was in fellowship with them. I really wanted to physically fight! I wanted my son back. He always loved his father and had high hopes of making it big one day. But the price tag was too high. When the pastor he was playing for moved out of state, so did my son, along with other church members.

We continued to bind the spirit that had my son. I had gotten so sidetracked with praying for my son, I moved everything out of his bedroom and made it a prayer room.

God reminded me of all my children that were hurting too, and I wanted all of them saved and delivered in Jesus' name. Take back your authority over your children!

My mother was such a prayer warrior. We had such good things to say about her, especially when God took her home. But God said to me one day, "What will your children say about you? Have you lived your life of holiness before them?" Our son and daughters were true worshippers, even though the enemy thought he won.

Declare your children belong to God; never give in to the enemy! We love him, we talk to him, and the whole family went to visit him. We recognize the spirits that attack our family, as you must as well. Then cast them out by the power of God, and watch God move. Keep telling your children who they are and who they are going to be in the kingdom. I don't care if they hear your voice in jail, in the store, in the club, laying in a hotel room; God's word will not return void. He has made a promise to our children and yours too; the righteous seed!

I had to start spending more time with Ericka then; she was almost done with college at the time and needed us. Deidra was entering high school. Billy and Jevon were in middle school, so they needed our love and our wisdom, even if they didn't listen. We watched God turn the whole situation around; we now have a wonderful relationship with our son. We laugh and sometimes yet cry at what God has done. We knew we had to trust God to take care of him. Because he was in God's hands; just as the prodigal son returned and came to himself, so will your child.

God is faithful and watches over His word to perform it. The music ministry changed at our church, but you have to trust God through it all. Your faith will be tried to see if you believe His plan. We are accountable for how we portray Christ to our children. It took years, but I finally dedicated a room for prayer for my family. The room is anointed, even walking past the door. The room was sacred and a safe place because salvation is free. The children could also go in for prayer.

Find a place for God in your house to warfare for your children; the attack on their entire generation is great, but God is greater. Also, keep your word to your children; whatever you say you're going to do, try your best to do it.

I shared this story about my son and children because sometimes we were so busy doing other things that the enemy could creep in unaware; our son did amazing things in the music industry! We are so proud of him. Keep loving your children unconditionally! That's the love of Christ they will see.

Most of all, don't let church people dictate how you should raise your children! They can't run their own home. That's between you and your husband and God.

We have pushed thousands of children away from the cross with foolishness. They have a soul too. Our children tell us now, "Thank you for being the parents you were!" They always say they hear me say wherever they are, "You are the Righteous Seed! You will never fit in Your Royalty."

Bought and Paid For

There are many things that really bother me in the kingdom now. I have had the pleasure of knowing and being acquainted with some beautiful holy women of God! Some have transitioned to glory, and others are waiting to be picked up. I had a dear mother in the Lord in my life.

That special mother, even though she was not a pastor's wife, was a pioneer that stood for holiness and righteous living and imparted wisdom in my life along the way. What I'm about to share now worries me…

"Every wise woman buildeth her house: but the foolish plucketh it down with her hands" (Proverbs 14:1).

We are living in a day where some women are in competition with their mates, and they have humiliated them in public and in private. They belittle their spouse in front of the children and congregation. They refuse to let him lead the house, and she be the guide. This type of woman talks about her husband and their problems with the children. The children have no respect because their mother shows no respect.

This type of woman deprives her husband of any sexual intimacy, and when she allows him to make love to her, it's degrading. By the way, the bed isn't the only place he desires to make love in. Stop telling him he didn't do it right! Ugh! I can't stand you. Fortunately for him, and unfortunately for you, somebody else will enjoy him down the road if you don't have the decency to.

This woman spends all the household finances on herself. This woman makes her husband feel he should be lucky to have her, which is further from the truth! This woman is what the Bible calls "foolish."

She has a good husband that supports the home, loves God and his family. He's quiet and meek and prayerful; he brings home his check, pays the bills, makes sound decisions…except he is troubled by the wife he has married.

He thought she was a little rough around the edges when they met but thought his love would melt her all the way down. It's been fifteen years now, and she's the worst!

This man of God needs a trophy, but what's really sad is he's lonely, hurt, feeling rejected, and despised. His foolish wife has opened the door of no return to the enemy's garden. Being a busybody, messy, arrogant, and full of pride, she ridicules him to her friends and family.

She does not have the Spirit of God abiding in her; if she did, God would show Himself to her and correct her. If this man continues to seek heaven regarding his marriage, it's going to draw her or drive her. In his case, it's a win-win.

This foolish woman felt like she didn't need to even communicate with him for accountability as to her whereabouts or anything. She was in control, but really, Satan was. She was rude, sarcastic, and never apologetic. As the plot thickens, guess what happens?

This woman got very sick, none of her so-called friends were there, who help her? Her husband, until she recovered.

So much damage had been done, they later divorced. This foolish woman, later on, wished she had her kind, loving spouse and yet criticized him for moving on. But all she did was trample him to the ground. Now she is cold and bitter. Remember, "Your trash is somebody else's treasure."

In the same regard, you have ungodly pastors that can't seem to keep their zipper up. My mother used to say, "They are saved from the waist up." How sad and true!

They are gifted men, and we are talking different denominations; yes, even COGIC. Their churches are full; their homes are bigger than a block, bank accounts in several places, garages for their expensive Bentley cars and jets. Several homes in different states. Closets bigger than most's entire homes. Their eyes are full, yet not satisfied! They will go out of town for revivals and holy convocations and meet up with their girlfriends and boyfriends too! They will literally sleep with both genders, many times the same day! They also have group sex with other fellow clergy and bishops.

Every man of God I see makes me wonder if they are faithful to God. If so, they will have no problem being faithful to their wives.

Some practice safe sex, even though there is no such thing as safe sex! It's a sin. They think they are considering their spouse, yet some are too freaky for a condom! "Bring it on, " they say! Meanwhile, they clean up and zip up and go portray being holy!

Many have beautiful wives that know about their Dr. Jekyll and Mr. Hyde husbands and have even confronted them. They have cried and traveled, but these preachers' wives will not give up that lifestyle! Their penthouse hotel suites when they travel; expensive clothes and jewelry, furs and diamonds. Yes, some of these wives are lesbians too. They also live private and separate lives! "Bought and paid for" couples blackmailing each other. Some are getting paid the minimum, not maxed of over $10, 000 a week! Imagine that. Instead of casting the devil out of your home, as in the days of old, he has a suite in your house!

Oh, not to mention some pastors are taking care of multiple homes, with women and men everywhere! What type of example will you leave for your children? Women are so stressed they are on prescription drugs, drinking, getting high; they can't cope! Jesus is still speaking, but they are enjoying being sneaky! What legacy are we leaving our children if we can be bought and sold like the world? Jesus bought us with a price, so we would not have to play the harlot!

The problem with being a servant to sin is you can't get out as quickly as you sell out. Bail has been posted, but your very being belongs to what you sold out to. It is going to take a sold-out life to Christ to return to the cross. Soul ties are real. You really are a prisoner of that sin. You think about it, dream about it; some will even die for it. Let go, and let God! Forgive yourself, and return to God. Whatever happened to alimony? These preachers' wives now demand payment to be your pulpit flower. "Pay up, and I'll shut up." But what they need to do is have an old fashion shut-in, pray and fast and watch God expose the spirit of witch-craft that has infatuated your home and ministry.

See, the Zion mothers would put Satan on the run, not entertain him in their home. You can take back what you gave away; you must fight for it. It may cost you everything, but if you really love God, it will be worth it. As a wise woman, you must tell your husband when he is wrong! You will never be able to gather the spirits that were unleashed during your times of disobedience in your home and ministry. There are consequences to disobedience! It's not okay to dance with demons! Secret lives are secret lies!

I really loved the story of Hosea that God command-ed him to go and buy her back time and time again. "**So I bought her to me for fifteen *pieces* of silver, and *for* a homer of barley, and a half homer of barley: And I said unto her, Thou shalt abide for me many days; thou shalt not play the harlot, and thou shalt not be for *another* man: so *will* I also *be* for thee**" (Hosea 3:2, 3).

So we would have an example of how He views the love that a husband shows to his wife, even when she doesn't want to be his wife! The example of Christ loving the church. Even when the church was in rebellion, God telling Hosea to marry a harlot was a symbol of what his Son Jesus was going to do for us, purchasing us back from the gates of sin.

We are the body that was bought and paid for through the blood of Jesus Christ only.

Surviving Loss

Years ago, when I married my husband, he was a holy guru. He was in constant fasting and praying and asking not to be disturbed. I felt lost most of the time. We were childless for two years, and he was always talking about getting ready to go to glory! So, I would say, "I'm going to be a widow already?" His reply would be, "God will take care of you." When we finally had Ericka, our oldest, he would fast (no food) for days, and I was a true housewife, taking care of the house and our infant. He would only come out of the room to bathe and use the restroom. He was in deep! He even had me laying on church floors, in shut-ins, and I was pregnant with Ericka! He was constantly in communion with God, preparing me for the loss of him, around for really anything. I was twenty years old, living like I was single. I really couldn't get furious; after all, he was with God. But oh, I was angry and neglected. I, too, was trying to live godly but really didn't understand the gifts God had placed in my life either. We were innocent babes in the Lord, seeking direction from Him.

We decided to enroll in Bible school to learn more about God. It was the best and worst of times. We learned a lot about our walk and met some amazing Christians along the way.

We didn't have much money, so we lived in the ghetto, had public assistance due to loss of employment, drove in cars that resembled the Flintstones due to holes being in the floor of the car. A young preacher's wife with no glamour at all. I was humiliated by my new life; it was not what I had imagined with the man of my dreams. Driving to church smelling like gasoline from the fumes in the car… It would have been over if somebody had struck a match. Yet, I made our house a home. I was very frugal; I shopped at second-hand stores, purchasing my husband's suits and my clothes. I even bought my first fur coat from a resale shop. I had to mentally support my husband when he lost jobs and would get depressed. I kept children and did hair out of the kitchen on the side to make ends meet. Much later in our life, we got college degrees and progressed financially. We bought homes and better cars and helped our children. But life happens, and so does loss. We had major deaths that really crippled us mentally and spiritually.

My mother's passing made me want to run from life and never look back. It took a God in heaven and hearing her voice for me to return; I had left everybody! I was furious at God! I figured I would get out while I could. God arrested me in the spirit; I could hear my mother as she would always say, "God don't let them slumber, nor sleep in their mess, trouble them." I couldn't get away from God.

Much later, we lost our home after filing bankruptcy; my husband was late on one payment! And our home went into foreclosure; it would not even sell. We left the home immaculate. We had to walk away from over eighty thousand dollars in equity. In a nice neighborhood, as well. We lived there for twelve years and raised our children there. My husband was inconsolable. Somehow, I shifted; I started looking for somewhere else to live, we still had the income.

I was not going to let our children see a sheriff come to our door! I found another home in another suburb, and we moved. I told my husband we can replace properties, not human life.

We were dealing with so much after that we began to quietly blame each other. I was getting bitter and went to get those divorce papers. I spoke to very few people about how I really felt.

Then, my sister invited us to come down to Illinois for Father's Day, so we drove down. I was miserable and felt

God had forgotten us; was I wrong? My sister, a real estate broker, said, "Let's go for a ride." It was raining. We went around the corner, and we saw a house she called. The lady invited us in and said she was ready to move!

Her husband was working out of state, and the house wouldn't sell. I was like, "I have to go get my husband." He came back and saw the house. We both liked the home. I applied for a teaching job and got hired shortly after. We went home and packed, and I moved to Illinois. Never looking back. My husband came a few weeks later. God made up to us in that house what we really lost. It was my secret desire to have that beautiful house.

My only regret was we really should have bought it when the market was upside down.

The bottom line is we have encountered different financial losses and have remained married!

It was very difficult at times. "For your shame *ye shall have double*; and *for* your confusion they shall rejoice in their portion: therefore in their land they shall possess the double: everlasting joy shall be unto them" (Isaiah 61:7).

That's enough to rejoice right there! We must speak the word over our life and every situation, regardless of if death situations are staring us in the face. The word of God is quick and powerful, sharper than a two-edged sword! We must sever with the sword the words of the enemy in the atmosphere. Decree and declare that God is a rewarder to all that seek Him!

But God told us not to put our trust in things that rust and perish. I would like to believe we have grown in these areas, and they have become teachable moments. I still believe in him and what God is going to manifest through him. I can't shake it. It's our dream. Sometimes, you share your dreams with the wrong people, and they become nightmares. Be careful who you sow into. The ground has to be rich soil to bring a harvest. That way you can survive whatever loss that's ailing you.

"I will restore the years that the locust hath eaten, the cankerworm, and the caterpillar, and the palmerworm, my great army which I sent among you" **(Joel 2:25).**

I'm so very thankful that God has honored my prayer in my youth; I never wanted to lose a child. Some of you may be dealing with that loss. God is a healer in that as well.

Seek help together so that God can mend you back together. It is a fact, due to Adam and Eve's disobedience to

God, the blame game still lives with couples today.

Do you forget who the author of confusion is? That wicked one Lucifer, Satan, the devil.

We blame each other and fight instead of blaming the spirit that brings the division. Fight the enemy! Your loved one is not your enemy.

I've seen couples lose houses they have built and companies too. For many, the shame was too much to survive the marriage, so they divorce. It's sad because you can recover from loss, but your spouse is not replaceable, even though many go and get a substitute.

"Likewise, ye husbands, dwell with them according to knowledge, giving honor unto the wife, as unto the weaker vessel, and as being heirs together of the grace of life; that your prayers be not hindered" (1 Peter 3:7).

Forget all the insulting statements the enemy will say to you; I should be further than this! I should have saved that money! I should, I should! I'm too old to be going through this!

Some people get depressed and commit suicide over stuff that you can go and buy again.

"Some trust in chariots, some in horses: but we will remember the name of the Lord our God" (Psalm 20:7). It's just stuff that can be replaced. We have discovered we must go on; whether we understand it or not, God has the perfect plan for our lives, and He can restore the years the locust and the palmerworm have eaten; He knew we would experience loss and would give us double for our shame.

Beauty for Ashes

"To appoint unto them that mourn in Zion, to give unto them beauty for ashes, the oil of joy for mourning, the garment of praise for the spirit of heaviness; that they might be called trees of righteousness, the planting of the Lord, that he might be glorified" (Isaiah 61:3).

First, I want to talk about the first woman God created, Eve. Not only was she the very first design God created for man, but she also experienced life and its consequences alone. Eve was the first woman to be married, without bridesmaids, anyone to help, do her makeup or hair; no father to give her away, no fancy white dress. Good thing she woke up in a garden where she had flowers already. Incidentally, when she woke up, there was Adam waiting for his new bride.

Remember, they were both naked and not ashamed! Eve was the first woman to get distracted by the enemy and get tricked and disobey God! How could she live this down, listening to the serpent?

Eve was the first woman that realized she was naked, and God made clothes for her. Eve was the first woman to give birth alone without midwives: who cut the baby's cord? Eve was also the first woman to bury her child, and have a funeral, and experience jealousy crueler than the grave with her other child.

Eve was also the first woman that lost two sons at once; one in death, the other a sentence that caused him to leave. Did Eve mourn? Of course, she did! But it's like everyone felt she deserved everything that happened to her because she disobeyed God! But how many times have we disobeyed God and have had to deal with the miserable consequences?

Eve also used the blame card; it didn't matter that Adam was taking a mental nap while she was being beguiled. It became her fault for listening. Eve, to me, was the first preacher's wife. She had a lot of responsibility, as the women today. Adam had to name all the animals, watch the garden; forbidden to go here or there, like a shepherd but got distracted from the will of God, which caused him and us our birthright.

Eve lost her husband's confidence and trust in her; can you imagine their life after that?

We know from being married his resentment towards her. She made a mistake that made Jesus come down to correct! You know how, when we make mistakes, it takes a long time for situations to simmer down. We all play the blame game. Some couples divorce from the humiliation of it all. Adam and Eve couldn't; they didn't even know what divorce was.

Some wives have had to mourn publicly instead of privately the deaths of their husbands, children, parents. Perhaps mere death sentences of imprisonment, children with incurable diseases, mental illness, etc. How can we find *beauty for ashes*? God said we could. Beauty can come from many sources. Your beauty could be your stature in the midst of adversity. Your Beauty could be the salvation of the Lord. Your beauty could be having the strength in mourning to get up and dress up; "beautifying" yourself when you've cried till your eyes are swollen.

Beauty can also come from God's grace and mercy to look and see beauty in a pile of ashes; "From what?" you might say. A bitter divorce because of your child being molested by her father.

A parent suffering from Alzheimer's or dying with cancer. What beauty? The beauty is to be able to love them from life to death, perhaps to thank them for being wonderful parents, having the beauty to comfort them, and pray with them through the transition. Holding and bathing them.

From ashes, knowing God saved my life one night. I was sixteen, up studying for my driver's test the next day. I removed the shade from the lamp to see and fell asleep. I was awakened by my sister, lying in a burning bed, and I could have slept away from the thick black smoke. Having the daily reminder of the smell of the fire, but yet not being harmed by the fire, being alive and not dead.

Some have lost a child, whom no one can replace; yet, you mourn the day they passed as well as their birthday. The beauty is that God gave you time to share your life and love with that child.

Even though we grieve and mourn, God wants us to see His beauty through the windows of smothering fiery hot ashes and yet give thanks in it all.

When my mother passed, I didn't see any good in it. I was thirty-two years old at the time. I felt robbed and deprived, especially when I saw other mothers and daughters together. Then one day, I realized I was blessed to have her as long as I did. Some women lost their mother at childbirth, at adolescent ages, teen years, etc. At least, she was able to see my children, hold them, and pray for them.

Some are mourning abortions from years ago; forgive yourself and move on.

Our youngest sister was expecting her first child when our mother passed. Even though my mother helped name him, she never got to physically be there for his birth, her daughter's first child's birth, or her marriage.

It was a great loss for her being only twenty-three years old. She had not yet finished developing. There is nothing like a mother's love, so I learned to appreciate those thirty-two years! It's been over twenty years. We still miss her—all six of her children and grandchildren.

My peace and rest are that she is with Jesus, and that's where I want to be when it's time. Make no mistake about it, we as children of God have forgotten to live each day like it's our last, loving people right, treating people right. Not speaking idol words, telling somebody about your Savior, so they can see His face in peace. There is life after death; all the crying in the world won't change that. How we treat one another is the key. God can dry your tears and help you to see beauty through the ashes! Some make excuses for being mean-spirited, "You don't know what I've been through!" If you don't get it right on this side of heaven, a liar won't be able to tarry in His sight.

Whatever pill of bitterness and blame you carry, we must bring our spirits of heaviness to the cross to eliminate the weight that cripples our destiny in Him. Today we ask God to heal our hearts from grief and disappointments. Let the breath of God blow on us, wiping away the ashes, so we can see and feel His beauty to live and not die through the storms of life.

Authentic Me

Recently, I was listening to my pastor's wife speaking for Mother's Day. During her introduction, she mentioned what you see is what you get, "authentic me." Of course, that got me thinking about how she has said her husband has always allowed her to be herself and evolve and how she thanks him for that! From my account, I applaud him for being different at a time when male chauvinism was big in our churches.

I can't tell you how many wives had to be the Barbie in the box, with all her many attachments and job descriptions. Barbie was glamourous, you could sit her anywhere, and she looked amazing; sit her near a piano, and she'd play; give her a microphone, and she would sing. Place her in the kitchen to cook and clean and so on. That's where the Stepford Wives arrive from. Beautiful women at your beck and call, and very submissive.

"I will praise thee; for I am fearfully and wonderfully made: marvelous are thy works; and that my soul knoweth right well" (Psalm 139:14).

The first problem with Barbie is that's not my name!

Second, it's an insult to want a prototype woman. It's an insult to God that made us unique and different. All of us can't sing and play the piano to help build your church up, but we can do other things if you would allow the Holy Spirit to deal with you about what's in your own house.

One of the most profound things my husband ever told me, when we were pastoring together, was that he was praying for a house prophet, and God told him that he had one already! My husband asked God who. And He said, "Your wife." Imagine that what he was looking for was already in the house! Oftentimes, leaders put other women preachers they feel are more knowledgeable over their wives, perhaps to teach them the homiletics of preaching or teaching, etc.; the pastor feels they are so anointed and can teach you something.

I was at a conference some years back, and that's exactly what the other associated pastor got up and said, almost bragging how she's teaching the first lady how to present herself before God's people. I was confused! The ministry now is huge, but when it was growing, who was there supporting her husband when they struggled financially, inventing meals with barely three ingredients? No proper wardrobe, borrowing clothes and money, yet maintaining a home and the children and having relations with the husband while he was cash broke! Who taught her how to speak, then? I have a problem with the pastor forgetting who has been in that pressure cooker with you. Sorry, sweetie, I'm not ashamed to say that pastor will never have the anointing that's on his wife's life! Because that came from God and long-suffering and prayer.

Be careful how you measure your coins, your treasure in earthen vessels who walk beside you. Don't get overtaken by somebody else's charm. God gave you, man of God, everything you need to succeed.

Barbie is fake, and these days what you might be trying to trade your wife in for may be fake! Fake eyes, fake breasts and hips. Sorry to say, Frankenstein lives; they can even reproduce sexual organs. I said that nicely. So, you really don't know what you're getting. All these spiritual women you might be admiring don't prefer men anyway!

Open your spiritual eyes so you can see it. We definitely can! Never underestimate your mate. Women, stop being predictable, always do something different, be creative. Everything doesn't require money, even though it's nice to have. Pastors, I love you so much and the office that you're desperately trying to represent. Many of you are awesome.

But for the others, get Barbie out of the shoebox underneath your arm. Your wife is not a pulpit flower! She is loaded with all the power you will need. One day, we will be in a box and won't have any knowledge of being there because we will be dead.

Deliver us from our living boxes. Encourage us to grow, ask us what God has shown us to do in ministry and how you can assist her in that development. We both want the same thing, to please God! Eve was the very first, first lady in essence, and by all accounts, Adam was just as important as the president of the United States. Remember, he had dominion over every creature; in fact, he named them. No greater privilege did Eve have as the first woman, perfected for that one man! Eve also made the first mistake that cost us all our birthright. But how many mistakes have we made? She simply had to forgive herself daily.

Eve teaches us the real role of a wife. If she had been more prayerful, she could have stood up to the serpent and said, "God can not lie!" How are our lives different? It's because she forgot who she was! This is why so many wives struggle with self-esteem issues. God doesn't make mistakes! Woman of God, you were chosen to do this. You were created to be his wife! You can buck or bow in submission to the will of God for your life. I know how hard it is, with tears in my eyes even now writing this. But God is faithful concerning His word.

"Come unto me, all ye that labor and are heavy laden, and I will give you rest. Take my yoke upon you, and learn of me; for I am meek and lowly in heart: and ye shall find rest unto your souls. For my yoke is easy, and my burden is light" (Matthew 11:28-30).

Husbands, we need your confidence in us; no matter how long you have been married, tell us we are doing a good job in ministry. Tell her she is beautiful every day, especially on Sunday. That's the day some women dress specifically to get your attention. If your wife hasn't gotten your attention, somebody else will give it. Please fill in all the gaps so Satan can't come in. Keep your love and your fists tight.

"Be sober, be vigilant; because your adversary the devil, as a roaring lion, walketh about, seeking whom he may devour" (1 Peter 5:8).

Thank her for being the love of your life. And, wives, please take care of your husbands! Tell them they still look good, smell good, feel good. Wives, you know what to do.

Sorry to tell you, church is not safe. Being in the will of God is *safety*. This other stuff is other stuff. No other voice should have and speak more volumes than your wife. When God is let into the church again, then we will become the brides of Christ. Until then, we will have bench fillers that come to church for no other reason than to conquer and divide. We must get back to pure holiness. When spirits enter the sanctuary, they are too uncomfortable to stay without repentance.

Sorry to say, this is not just females but also males that are in hot pursuit of the first family! Most women are not insecure but can't help that they see that spirit when it comes in the room. If the world has enough sense to guard the first family with the Secret Service because of threats, what's wrong with the church?

"But as it is written, Eye hath not seen, nor ear heard, neither have entered into the heart of man, the things which God hath prepared for them that love him" (1 Corinthians 2:9).

Zion has been rocked to sleep with a demonic sedative! It's time to wake up and be about our Father's business. We can't keep hugging venous snakes and think they will be okay and not bite us and kill us. Nope, the enemy has to flee; there is only one place for him; get out!

We have to fall back in love with Christ and allow God to give us a praying spirit. We are so distracted by our phones and devices and every gadget in our lives that have become idols.

We, too, must repent and make time for our Father to speak to us and help us to guard our man of God and family through prayer and supplication. The fight is not physical; it's spiritual warfare. We truly need the whole armor of God. We must work while it is day because when night comes, it's over.

Finally, my brethren, be strong in the Lord, and in the power of his might. Put on the whole armor of God, that ye may be able to stand against the wiles of the devil. For we wrestle not against flesh and blood, but against principalities, against powers, against the rulers of the darkness of this world, against spiritual wickedness in high places. Wherefore take unto you the whole armor of God, that ye may be able to withstand in the evil day, and having done all, to stand. Stand therefore,

having your loins girt about with truth, and having on the breastplate of righteousness; And your feet shod with the preparation of the gospel of peace. Above all, taking the shield of faith, wherewith ye shall be able to quench all the fiery darts of the wicked. And take the helmet of salvation, and the sword of the Spirit, which is the word of God:

Praying always with all prayer and supplication in the Spirit, and watching thereunto with all perseverance and supplication for all saints.

Ephesians 6:10-18

Amen to the Word of God!

My Sister's Keeper

I am my sister's keeper. We are supposed to protect each other as Ruth did Esther. We can also expose wrongdoings when we see them. When I began journaling this book some years ago, there was not a lot of technology that exists today. Pagers were big back then, and growing up, the telephones were on the wall. Whatever was going on, you waited until you got home to talk. We now have so many issues in the church world. You can snap a picture on your phone, and it goes viral.

Now, wives are catching husbands on the show *Cheaters*, running husbands over with their cars; wives literally killing their husbands, leaving the children fatherless and motherless. Even husbands are fighting their wives... Incidentally, no one expects you to stay in an abusive relationship; run for your life!

Wives are also catching husbands in bed with not only women but also men. Husbands are being public successes and private failures. What happens when the preacher divorces his wife for his mistress?

"Righteousness exalteth a nation: but sin is a reproach to any people" (Proverbs 14:34).

What happens to the wife when the mistress exposes publicly her affair because he won't leave his wife? Can we imagine the wife's shame and humiliation? Everything she decides is ultimately her decision. Even if she decides to stay and pray for her man of God.

We are also living in a day where disease is rampant and incurable. I remember when venereal disease (VD) was the stuff growing up in health class. Now, there are incurable diseases everywhere to be careful of.

Wives must be wise these days. I know of a man that had an affair unknowingly with a woman that had full-blown AIDS, and she boasted to his wife she would have him, and he died.

Many preachers have outside children; some deny it, others look at it as a medal. But the children always showed up with their bold mothers at the funeral to pay their respect. Chaos!

Some pastors sleep with every needy woman in the church that lets them. Some gracious pastors are having mental affairs with the church as the other woman. So devoted they forget their wives come first! Then, the church:

God knew what he wanted for the family. We change the God-given order, then wonder why there is disorder! If only, as women, we would sound the alarm the moment something is out of place. There would not be so much adultery and fornication. Some you see have not married in the cloth, so they can continue to clearly be inappropriate.

I am my sister's keeper; most wives feel something is wrong, but many times can't face it. The hurt and betrayal might be closer than you think.

Please read: **"And he went in also unto Rachel, and he loved Rachel more than Leah, and served with him yet seven other years" (Genesis 29:30).**

Let's go to the word. What we are presently dealing with started centuries ago with Rachel and Leah; these were biological sisters. Now, Leah knew that Jacob was Rachel's man, yet she was hot in her flesh, not good to look upon; she conspired with her father to take her sister's husband. It didn't stop there; once Jacob found out he had been tricked, Leah figured she could make him forget her sister by lathering him up with her lovemaking. However, Laban agreed to give Rachel to Jacob at the end of the week.

I can't imagine how Rachel felt, being betrayed by her father and sister and having to keep quiet. The competition

began; Leah began to have babies while Rachel was barren.
Leah had six sons and one daughter. So, guess what Rachel
did because Leah kept bragging? Rachel offered Jacob to
wife her handmaiden Bilhah, and she had children. Then
Leah got jealous and offered her handmaid to Jacob, to wife
Zilpah, and she had sons. Wow, all this trickery and sin.
Then finally, God heard Rachel and opened her womb, and
she bared Joseph. One sister started out sharing her hus-
band with her sister and two handmaids. That's where the
Mormon religion gets their rights to share.

Jacob didn't complain; he was more than willing to sat-
isfy these wives. So let's not wonder where this spirit came
from.

**"Now Sarai Abram's wife bore him no children:
and she had a handmaid, an Egyptian, whose name was
Hagar" (Genesis 16:1).** We also have Sarah, who bought
in the spirit of the mistress. Jacob married those handmaids.
But because Sarah disobeyed God, Hagar called Sarah her
"mistress." It's interesting how, once again, Satan took that
word for a wife, "mistress, " and transformed it to another
woman. Sarah offers her handmaid later to be his wife;
Abraham was in Canaan for ten years.

Sarah was specific, have a child! Not a fling, a child.

Then she got jealous. Why?

All of this got good to Abraham. You took a good man—he had to be good, ladies, because she even called him Lord!—but made him a consenting adulterer. The power of a woman, even in disobedience. Just think of our power if we were obedient. Now we have a nation; God didn't intend for Abraham to seed.

We have an awesome task. We can make or break a ministry that God has given our men of God. Watch who you share all your secrets with and to. Some people are there just to get close to the pastor through you.

Some of you need to carry your own Bible; all these armor bearers are not disciplined to walk where you have been and where God is taking you. They are too carnal. I'm not saying they have to be deep, but they should be deep enough to labor and pray for you. Not being a busybody and looking for all your house secrets so they can go tell everybody that has an ear.

Many years ago, as a housewife, I got a job as a housekeeper for a very prominent basketball player for the Milwaukee Bucks; his wife was a local news anchor. My responsibilities were to clean, cook, wash, iron, etc. In a twenty-two-plus room house. Everything was at my disposal. No room was off-limits. I cleaned the whole house. I organized and saw the costs of bills, etc. But I valued my job, so I didn't run them down. It was a great opportunity into a world I had strived for.

I later resigned because I found out we were expecting our second child (Eric II). But my reputation was so good I could have returned. Every job I have had, I served with integrity, especially in the church. No one could do my job better. I love it.

We should know how to serve God's people without lowering our underwear. Our posture should be in the presence of the Lord. I have heard of the abuse of leaders, locking their church office door, placing women over their desk, and getting in a quickie before the sermon. Not their wives!

Outrageous, one of those men died a fool. His wife found him in bed out of town with another's man's wife.

This has become an epidemic in our churches. Some wives know their husbands are freaks and have consorted with them in a threesome so they won't lose him. Now the church is a mess. How are we going to win when they are lost?

Furthermore, then we beseech you, brethren, and exhort you by the Lord Jesus, that as ye have received of us how ye ought to walk and to please God, so ye would abound more and more. For ye know what commandments we gave you by the Lord Jesus. For this is the will of God, even your sanctification, that ye should abstain from fornication :That every one of you should know how to possess his vessel in sanctification and honor; Not in the lust of concupiscence, even as the Gentiles which know not God: That no man go beyond and defrauds his brother in any matter: because that the Lord is the avenger of all such, as we also have forewarned you and testified. For God hath not called us unto uncleanness, but unto holiness.

1 Thessalonians 4:1-7

Now, this is tight, but it's right. This is not to the true men and women of God serving Him with all their hearts. This book represents imposters in the body of Christ, and somebody has to be bold enough; to tell the truth without naming names. I got a few, but that's not the point; God said: "Marriage *is* honorable in all, and the bed undefiled: but whoremongers and adulterers God will judge" (Hebrews 13:4).

"Cry aloud, spare not, lift up thy voice like a trumpet, and shew my people their transgression and the house of Jacob their sins" (Isaiah 58:1).

Did you catch that, Jacob? Need I say more? The only place that speaks about the truth, but doesn't want to hear the truth, is the church! I am on assignment to do this. God speaks to me everywhere, and I have to stop what I'm doing and write.

So, whether I want to or not, I'm being obedient to Him. We have got to get back to holiness instead of coming to church like you are doing the pastor a favor. No, God did you a favor; He woke you up. Cover your family!

Let's continue to pray and cover our sisters in Christ so we will please our heavenly Father.

The Practice Church

Let's talk about those godly preachers that love God with all their heart and whose only focus was to please God and make Him proud. We have so many examples: Billy Grahams, Oral Roberts, Rex Hubbard, RW Shambach, EG Hill, Bishop Charles Harris Mason, and many more. These were public pastors and evangelists that were determined to do ministry or die trying.

Many of these men were gone from home for weeks to months at a time. And when they came home: they made babies and left again. As if God didn't know they had a wife and children. They felt God would be displeased in them if they stayed home too long. Some pastors were gone so long they forgot how to be husbands. Coming home made them irritated, agitated, and uncomfortable. Some would say, "That old wife you gave me, Lord, I just don't understand. I must be about kingdom ministry." Many were just pure evangelists. However, God gave them a practice church, which was his wife and family! **"For if a man knows not how to rule his own house, how shall he take care of the church of God?" (1 Timothy 3:5)**

Now, let's look again. God wanted him to learn how

to love and communicate with his family; how to instruct his home, and not with an iron fist. **"Husbands, love your wives, even as Christ also loved the church and gave himself for it" (Ephesians 5:25).**

I recently interviewed two pastors who have been pastoring for a while now. So I asked them what their expectations for a preacher's wife were. One said, "To help me in ministry; even though she said, 'God didn't call me, He called you.'" Sad to say that was my favorite thing to say. But, woman of God, you too are called because you are one. The enemy comes in to cause us to separate who and what we are.

Our role is supportive and foundational, or it could not stand; I knew that the question would make them think. I also asked them, "Does your tone of voice change when speaking to your wife?" One pastor said, "I'm working on that." He was so honest because it is important. If we are, in fact, the practice church, we too are like sheep. But many have gone to the slaughter. **"Yea, for thy sake are we killed all the day long; we are counted as sheep for the slaughter" (Psalm 44:22).**

I notice that, even if a pastor is upset or distracted, they still watch how they speak to the sheep. Their audible tone is different; even in correction, it's loving. How do you speak to your wife and children? What does it sound like? Are you all frowned up when you answer your wife's questions? When your wife calls your name, do you say, "What?" Or "Yes, dear?" We are your practice church. God did give you a manual; it's called the Bible.

I would ask my husband, when our home was full of children, to change his tone so they could not only listen but trust him. Everything can't go from zero to a hundred. You push your family away. Guess what? They will resent you later. They, too, have souls and watch how well you treat the other church. We cannot have modern-day Jekyll and Hydes. For the wives, it is the worst, like making love without intimacy. Yuk. We need loving tones, yes, even in correction.

My husband was always correcting me long before he pastored because he, too, wanted to please God. Before he knew better, he would say, "If you don't act right, God will remove you." I can laugh now, but I couldn't then. What we both didn't understand was we were the practice church.

I see pastors desperate for church growth, but has their God-given practice church given you any fruit and growth for your labor?

Some men of God speak to their wives rudely in public; some confide in other women about their wives and church, which is the beginning of sorrow.

Some husbands run their wives like a thoroughbred racehorse. Some wives work harder than a mule. Many of these women die before their husbands can even apologize. Thanks be to God; they will get their reward in the arms of Jesus.

Your family should be the picture of God's church. Everything won't be perfect, but your love and guidance will be. There is everything now sitting in the pews. But we continue to show God's love and preach Christ crucified.

Stop thinking that the family God gave you is embarrassing; He was getting you ready for real embarrassment. Being a leader is humbling. It will not always be the best people in town, but you still have a mandate to lead.

"And whosoever shall exalt himself shall be abased; and he that shall humble himself shall be exalted" (Matthew 23:12).

If we blame each other, we beat the wrong enemy. Your family is not the enemy.

Many times, the husband causes strife in his home,

comparing his family with Pastor Buckhorn across town. Nurture the garden God gave you; it will grow. Speak tender to your wife.

"Likewise, ye husbands, dwell with them according to knowledge, giving honor unto the wife, as unto the weaker vessel, and as being heirs together of the grace of life; that your prayers be not hindered" (1 Peter 3:7). For us, it validates us; it speaks love and affirmation to our spirits and hearts. When you get it right, we become heirs together, and our prayers are not hindered. Wow. That other stuff sends rejection; we were built to absorb your love and kindness.

"Wives, submit yourselves unto your own husbands, as unto the Lord. For the husband is the head of the wife, even as Christ is the head of the church: and he is the savior of the body. Therefore, as the church is subject unto Christ, so let the wives be to their own husbands in everything" (Ephesians 5:22-24).

Wives, no greater voice should be followed than our husband's; we too must submit being the neck so the head can move much smoother. There is only one voice we honor: our husband. Besides God, anything else with two heads is a monster.

I am thoroughly convinced God gives pastors, in their homes, everything they need to be successful, in their wives and children. The problem arises when they look for another to fulfill the emptiness that they have ignored, by many times shutting her out. Frustration sets in. The enemy will tell you, "She just doesn't understand; she doesn't have my back. She wants to hinder my ministry." Really? Your wife is your ministry; get that right. God holds you responsible.

Some powerhouse men would not even run over an animal on the street but can't seem to find your address on that same street. God gave you a clue, men, when He said, "Love your wife like Christ loved the church!" Hello, it's the practice church.

I just watched a pastor doing a vow renewal service for his children. As he began to weep, he said, "I've been married for over sixty years. I was a wonderful pastor and a horrible husband!" Why? They thought God had amnesia or something. God saw the ministry before you did. He knew you had a wife before you married her. Imagine that.

"Before I formed thee in the belly I knew thee; and before thou camest forth out of the womb I sanctified thee, and ordained thee a prophet unto the nations" **(Jeremiah 1:5).**

Yes, even before you were born, the only person in the trick bag is us from Satan. That's why God gave her to you; to help you. That's where trouble starts; please don't find joy and solace talking to other women because you feel they are so anointed and profound! Really, so is your wife. She has to be to stay married to you. I say that respectfully, but go figure.

Wives, we have to continue to lift our husbands up in prayer. When I married my husband, I had the right package; everything was where it should have been. Some years later, many things happened: from pastors to bishops hitting on me; something happened to my mind, mentally, and I'm just admitting to it. I allowed my beautiful self to gain weight and look less desirable like it was all my fault. It wasn't.

Since I had a past of sexual abuse, it was easy to hide and feel trapped, so I developed lumps and bumps all over trying to hide. But I didn't even think about my husband losing his eye candy because I caught myself hiding it just for him.

Many years of regret and shame later, I'm facing that giant in my life called weight and everything associated with it. The enemy will have you wrap yourself up in someone's sin and call it yours.

The problem is whether I'm fat or thin when I walk into any room. I change the atmosphere, period. So I have decided to coldcock Satan and take my life and body back. I'm working so hard my husband is now telling me that I don't have to work out every day. My desire is still my own husband! I still enjoy serving him, fixing his plate, ironing his clothes, and preparing his clothes because that's not important to him; he doesn't care. But I do!

I learned from my father how to shine shoes, etc. The point is that there is nothing I would not submit myself to for him. I have some areas of my life I share with him, from the past sexually, that I tell him I will never like. But it has nothing to do with him, so we do different things to help me, help him.

"For it is a shame even to speak of those things which are done in secret" (Ephesians 5:12).

I believe in transparency, but it has not edified or helped the body of Christ, which is why my details will be limited. But my prayer to God was: "Lord heal me so I can be whole, " no person can do that but God. Also, conquering the fear and insecurities of another clergy because now I just tell them the wrong woman! I can also see that look when they struggle with that spirit. Actually, I had the gift before my experience, but I ignored it because I was young in the Lord and believed everybody was who they said they were. But every man of God I see, I wonder if they are saved for real, or if they only have waist up salvation, or if God is a part of every fiber of their being. I don't think they understand how much damage they cause abusing their clergy office. I used to love taking pictures but started taking headshots because a picture can't lie to you. I looked at a picture some years ago someone took of me and my dad, and I said, "Oh my God, I hate this picture." My father replied, "Why? It's you." He will simply tell you, "You are getting fluffy."

I was one of his daughters that was really thin. So he loved to tease me. But I remember when he questioned why and where I was going concerning that particular clergy. I was at a revival, and he called and said to get home to my husband! It's easy to get distracted serving; when wolves are all around you, and you're innocent, you will get bitten. Needless to say, my father was right!

"Her children arise up, and call her blessed; her husband also, and he praised her" (Proverbs 31:28).

Our greatest accomplishment as parents was when our

children told us, "Thank you for sticking it out and loving us and showing us Christ." Saints, that's worth it all.

I want to talk a little about the preacher that suffers from having wives that are flirty and have countless adulteress affairs. We have scripture to back it, Hosea and Gomer; she was a harlot, he had to buy her back!

Some pastors are so humble they feel they can't do any better. Many times, they were widowers that married younger women. They are ashamed but yet go on. One couple, I'm reminded of, had several businesses that kept the husband busy. So she could come on to the help like Potiphar's wife. Hotel visits, and only God knows where else. Burning with desire for someone's husband. Those women I call homewreckers, unapologetically! These women, like the men, rub their breasts against men walking by, or they wear very revealing clothing to get their attention.

The pastors are so hurt they either stay, devastated, or divorce only to hear the others say, "I told you so." Now, more than ever, we have suicide in the church; pastors are overwhelmed with their churches, forced to close, losing finances and their families. Some women can't handle their lifestyle changing, and they go and find another sugar daddy.

Pastors are putting guns to their heads and killing themselves or taking drug overdoses. Some will say, "How?" Simply put, once you get depressed, you get oppressed; then possession is at the door, and you will entertain all Satan brings because you're too spiritually weak to fight.

In my life, through many disappointments, I attempted suicide twice! The last time was shortly after my mother passed. I was so angry, so depressed, and humiliated by secrets uncovered that backsliding wasn't enough. I tried. But I wanted the pain to end. So I emptied out all my secrets too and said, "Forget it, I'm done; I never intended to hurt myself or anybody else." Yet, I was innocent and appeared guilty. So my husband was outside, painting the house, and I had a thing I would do: close our bedroom door and the curtains. I could hear the radio playing his favorite song, "I Believe in You and Me" by Whiney Houston. It spoke to the preacher. Our children were outside playing; I looked out and got some paper and simply wrote, "I'm sorry, and I love you." And then I swallowed all the pills I could find. I positioned myself in the bed as if I were in a coffin. I looked at the clock, and it was 1 p.m. and heard the phone ring, but I said to myself it's too late. Later, I found out it was my friend Donna. She kept calling. About the time my husband made it to the room, my breathing had gotten sporadic and heavy. He panicked to get the kids and ran across the street to see if the doctor on our block was home. He got me to the emergency room. When I woke up, I began to scream and cry because I was still alive! All my family was there and the police too!

They thought my husband was trying to assist me in the suicide because the time frame didn't match. So that same friend, Donna, had to tell the police what type of people we were. I could not even get released from the hospital without going through a mental health assessment. My sister said, "You better tell them you are stressed, or you will never get out."

The point I am making is that many women are depressed and take pills to get up and down while our mates go and nurse the other church. It was an eye-opener for my husband, of course; this was before he started pastoring. But I was a wreck, taking care of everybody else but myself. Needless to say, I wasn't praying because I was so angry. This is why it's so important when God places people in your heart. Stop, drop, and roll in prayer.

God used my friend that day to keep calling; it made my husband come into the house to check on me. Our prayers are powerful, but we negotiate with God saying "later" or "they are okay." They are not. Had I died that day, you would not be reading this book. If I could have mentally prayed, I would have done what Mama always said to me: "Debra, before you walk away from God, just begin to tell God, 'Thank you for all You have done, ' and if you finish and still want to leave, then leave." But what Mama knew that I didn't is you can't come to God with a grateful heart and not stay with Him! It's the same in our marriages; when we turn all our disappointments, mistakes, regrets into "Honey, I love you, I forgive you, " the situation changes.

You might have to suffer some consequences with the trials, but you can make it. Had I given up, I would have missed so much of the joy in my life: my spouse, my children, and now grandchildren. The enemy really is out to steal, kill, and destroy. We quote it, we read it, but we don't believe it will happen to someone we know.

Be Whole

This chapter will require some real honesty. One of my favorite quotes states: "To thine own self be true." Everybody has left and gone home, the curtains are down, we don't have to bow and blow kisses. No one is throwing flowers on the stage saying, "Encore, " and there's no applause. It's just us: me, myself, and I. At some point, God requires us to be alone and be okay. Not looking for extra company or voices of confirmation and acceptance. God just wants us!

"Behold, I will do a new thing; now it shall spring forth; shall ye not know it? I will even make a way in the wilderness, and rivers in the desert" (Isaiah 43:19).

"And when he putteth forth his own sheep, he goeth before them, and the sheep follow him; for they know his voice. And a stranger will not follow, but will flee from him; for they know not the voice of strangers" (John 10:4, 5).

There are times, as women of God when we silently require our husbands to fix things in us that only a God up in heaven can do. We look at them with strange discernment, like, aren't you a man of God? But they are not Chemist FrankenBibleman.

Many of us, if we could see our spirit man and all the baggage we carry around, we'd see it could fill up a room. I know when I would travel to convocations years ago at COGIC, I would have luggage for shoes, luggage for hats and purses. Coats because it was in Memphis back then. Luggage for church clothes and everyday clothes. Then travel books, etc. I haven't even mentioned luggage for my husband's stuff. And then, we drove. All this was before they started weighing luggage. We pattern our lives in the same way we have compartments for disappointments, compartments for unforgiveness, compartments for "this is your last chance to mess up." Compartments for all the times you were raped and why you have difficulty with your husband. Compartments for blaming each other for past financial mistakes. Compartments for "I like you, but don't love you." Compartments for excuses; compartments for complaints. You get the picture.

We have bags of luggage from which we can pick out what we want to wear that day or season, just like garments. We are supposed to put on the garments of praise, not pouting and complaining, as much as it hurts.

"To appoint unto them that mourn in Zion, to give unto them beauty for ashes, the oil of joy for mourning, the garment of praise for the spirit of heaviness; that they might be called trees of righteousness, the planting of the Lord, that he might be glorified" (Isaiah 61:3).

"Put on the whole armor of God, that ye may be able to stand against the wiles of the devil" (Ephesians 6:11).

We know that death and life are in the power of the tongue, but even when you don't speak it but portray it with our attitude: it's the same. It still cripples us from being whole. For those great bakers out there, can you make a pound cake without flour and eggs? God will not force us to be these wonderful preacher wives without the submission of our will. He is not a rapist, to put it plainly. He's a gentleman at the door, knocking, waiting to be invited in. God is not going to kick the door in to get to you. To perfect the recipe, He has for your life, that will require you to get rid of all that stuff.

If you choose to stay in your private room with all your luggage worth of excuses, He will sit by waiting with the oven hot, waiting to make you pure gold.

I don't know about you all, but I want God to get some

glory out of my life. All this suffering, shame, spiritual birth pains, etc.… I want His glory more than anything. So, for me, I had to be honest with myself. How and why did I permit myself to let myself go physically, with weight gain naturally, as well as spiritually?

I had to get to my root of reality; yours may be something different. But guess what? It's still baggage and weight.

"Wherefore seeing we also are compassed about with so great a cloud of witnesses, let us lay aside every weight, and the sin which doth so easily beset us, and let us run with patience the race that is set before us" (Hebrews 12:1). I love this scripture because I imagine we have a spiritual cheerleading squad, hoping we make it to the other side. But if we continue in excuses and strife with our luggage, it becomes sin; it upsets us, distracts us, prevents us from running the race! We are too tired and aggravated by the heavy load of luggage that we carry to every destination. We have not even considered seasons have changed in our lives, and most of the garments we can't even wear anymore, yet we drag them along with us. From home to home. Not even realizing how heavy they have gotten through the years. How can we be whole if we will not face what we were?

That's preventing us from becoming who we should be.

I heard a bishop say, "Why do we have a daily funeral for the mistakes in our life? If it's dead, have a funeral, and let it go!" I was recently asked, "How do I forgive the man that molested me as a child, and I was forced to keep silent because he was a close family member?" It broke my heart because I had the same thing happen to me.

At first, I paused, then I told this babe in the Lord to pray the Lord's prayer:

> **After this manner therefore pray ye: Our Father which art in heaven Hallowed be thy name. Thy kingdom come, thy will be done on earth, as it is in heaven.**
>
> **Give us this day our daily bread. And *forgive us our debts, as we forgive our debtors*.**
>
> **And lead us not into temptation, but deliver us from evil: For thine is the kingdom, and the power, and the glory *forever Amen.***

Matthew 6:9-13

At that moment, God gave me wisdom for what to say because not only does she want the offender to die, but she is struggling with a relationship with Christ because of the abuse. We have to accept the fact that people say, "Why didn't God stop this from happening to me? Or show my holy parents?" By the way, God did, but she was too afraid to tell her parents. After all, she was a child. He /She was still at blame, even if they deny it. We have to console the victim so they don't blame themselves for someone else's sickness. Believe the children, please parents. Everyone has to forgive themselves. It may not be easy, but necessary. To be whole.

This scripture has all that she needs to let it go and enjoy living her life. People can say whatever they want, but it does affect your life, your relations with your spouse, people, period! Yet, we must stop looking like a bag lady in the spirit, with a shopping cart carrying all our stuff. It's spring cleaning; let's let it go. In this case, we can't give it away, and we must destroy it.

I remember, as a young wife, I kept diaries, and I would compare my husband to my past and all my complaints down through the years. One day, in prayer and fasting, the Lord revealed to me to get rid of them! For a couple of reasons, one, I didn't want something to happen to me and my children if they found them and read how I struggle to be happy and content. Second, my husband didn't deserve to be compared to whomever else. As he would call it, the soap opera world. The word of God clearly tells us in the book of Corinthians, "Love keeps no record of wrong!" So why do we keep mental records? We have issues with trust because of our luggage. Some of our luggage is ripping and smelling like mildew; it's so old. Yet we carry it.

My discovery was that if a man or woman is faithful to God, they will be faithful to you. So, we are responsible for ourselves. We must yield our members to the creator, so we can be completely whole, content, and pure before the King.

"I beseech you therefore, brethren, by the mercies of God, that ye present your bodies a living sacrifice, holy acceptable unto God, which is your reasonable service" **(Romans 12:1).**

Just like we have learned to travel these days with just a carry-on because we don't want to pay extra dollars at the airport, we must learn how to carry all our luggage to the King! Casting all our cares on Him because He cares for us. Most of us love valet service and concierge at fine hotels, to carry all our luggage, as we walk through the hotel, with our heads high as people whisper, "Who is that?" Well, that's how the Holy Spirit wants to brag to the enemy about us! How we surrendered it all to the Spirit of the living God to boast, "I'm carrying all their luggage and weight that's too heavy and upsets them."

God reminds us we are royalty and would never be seen carrying luggage and weight too heavy for us to carry. It all belongs to the Master King, Jesus!

Glory to God, in the highest, for lifting us far above any situation that we face.

As we surrender to a Holy God, making better choices, we can rest knowing our spirit man is healthy and whole. As the songwriter says, "Open my eyes, help me believe I am what you see. You see me victorious and rejoicing. That I survive not lame, but heal and whole."

The Puppet Master

This chapter has been brewing in my spirit like no other. I really wanted to be careful not to offend anyone, but I'm at a crossroads of decision again. I was talking with my husband about the church we grew up in; back when church was not as complicated. I thought about when secretaries counted the money at the table; the deacons would unfold, and she would let you know how much more money was needed. I remember hearing our pastor say, "That's table money! Don't ask the people for that." My things have changed. We can text our offerings, pay online; there are machines in the church foyer, credit card lines during offerings, etc. We are technology gurus in the church. We have big screens to watch and film, we have large choirs and live bands for our entertainment. We have praise dancers, mime dancers, the best of theater and arts; we have drama teams, we have greeters at our doors, adjutants, deacons, armor bearers, cupbearers, personal chefs, drivers, housekeepers in the church, and so on. We are in the best and worst of times. Yet, the church is still aching for deliverance and healing. We tell people what time to meet, what time to greet, how long to fellowship. How long to sing, how long to pray. Let's get the people happy and emotional and feel good, then let's do an offering! People are tired of being a puppet. God Himself, in many of our sanctuaries, is still standing outside of the church, waiting for an opportunity to come in. We are so rehearsed it's sickening. I'm not talking about the order in the house that's needed. I'm speaking of your plan for each and every planned service, not God's. When can He speak? When was the last time you really sought God for a real word? I'm at my end with church as usual. I'm not a puppet! The church is playing games. It might as well be a carnival. Especially the Holiness church that depended on God to speak and move. Zion, what's wrong? And if this has to be my platform to cry out, then I will. Wail and mourn for the daughters of Zion.

A pastor just recently eulogized our cousin's funeral and mentioned that in Milwaukee, Wisconsin, 76 percent of people there are not attending church. Yet we run over the church outside to get inside of a building to recycle saints that have been to everybody's church! We are losing an entire generation because they are turned off of church and because all they see are street games. That's what angers me as a preacher's wife, watching so many disappointing situations in our churches.

Our grown children, in their thirties, are having conversations with us now about whom they believe in. How they hate religion. We strive to tell them the word of God and stress it's a relationship, not religion. But what about my frustration as well? The church has changed so drastically that we have been in the church our whole lives, and have been serving God for over thirty years, and have questions as well. Thank God I understand the word of God and all the things that have to happen in these last days. Even though the church has the advantage to be explosive spiritually in this last hour, many are drawn away in their own lusts. Money has become their God, ungodliness in the pulpit with promiscuity in the pews. I said it and refuse to take it back! Will the real men of righteous integrity please stand up? The church is pacifying everybody's weakness as if the blood does not work. Jesus gave his life so we could have eternal life without strings attached like a puppet. His love was unconditional. We make excuses for people not being delivered and free and give them the keys to run ministries.

I simply don't recognize the church. We have more than hearts can wish for, and we want to bargain with God. No, He wants our life; it's our reasonable service.

We want to be seen in the best clothing, the best homes

and cars; travel here and there, have your team leading behind you looking important; yet nobody on that team can cast out a spirit! Why? I'll tell you: is it because they belong to the puppet master? They have the look and sound, but their soul is dehydrated; nothing is there but a form of godliness. We sit in churches on Facebook, our children watching video games, etc. How will they understand and hunger for God when you are giving them distractions right while the word of God is going on?

Our children have no respect for the house of God because we don't respect His house. If death would come back in the church house, order would come, then. People coming in, around, and outside, committing murder in our churches Why? Nobody can pray long enough inside the sanctuary to get discernment, which is part of being warned by God! God is sick of agendas that don't include Him. I am convinced the church needs to repent, regardless of what faith is outside of your door. Righteousness exalts a nation, and sin is a reproach to any people. We see it every day. Pastors, bishops, apostles, and any other big name they desired; they divorce their wives or have girlfriends on the side and then mount the pulpit.

I call them masters of disguise. Let's not mention, many

have other sexual partners, as well. Some will never get married because they enjoy being puppet master, using their black book for women and men. Now I know we all have our interpretation of what a church should be and look like. But we need to go back to what the word is requiring from us. I recently heard a pastor say, "God is going to have to give my wife something to do in ministry because I know what to do." I said, "She is already doing her job! Standing by you, covering you, praying for you, loving you. We don't have to be in some sort of sport against you. I am you!" We cannot be your puppet either; it's time to cut the strings; God gave everyone the free will to choose.

We are intelligent people, not idiots. We are not puppets made of wood. He wasn't real. We have an entire generation that really is not concerned with knowing our God.

"And also, all that generation were gathered unto their fathers: and there arose another generation after them, which knew not the Lord, nor yet the works which he had done for Israel" (Judges 2:10).

It is our responsibility to bring Christ back into our congregations, where they feel convicted to repentance. I praised God for the pastors that are yet on the wall without being distracted with this end-time church. That tells you,

Dock, you don't have to work that hard, preach this way, do this and that. But if that's not what God has instructed you to do, you are sinning.

"Therefore, to him that knoweth to do good, and doeth it not, to him it is sin" (James 4:17).

We will have no excuses when we stand in front of judgment day. I will not have God tell me, "Depart, I never knew you!" That verse gets me.

The church has slandered other clergy and is too proud to ask for God's forgiveness because they think they are right, but, in fact, the puppet master is in control of your being.

We really need a word from the Lord to remove all doubt. It's praying time. I'm not talking about you rehearsing prayers where the spirit can't come in, but rather laying prostrate on the floor until we hear God speak; until our spirits are broken from the world, until our children feel God's anointing, moving through the house.

I remember growing up years ago, and the older saints could tell if you had been spending time with the Lord. They would say your face is glowing, like Moses' face when he was with the Lord. Now people tell you when they fast; that's not the word. You have your reward. You can't fast and still be mean as a devil. Having a disciplined life means demons know who you are and tremble at the name of Jesus.

Just in case you're wondering who the puppet master really is: it's Satan. He is the one that causes us to deter from the true plan of holiness. He's cunning. He will make you think it's your idea, but it's his influence, even if it comes from another clergy. Seek God, not the wisdom of men. It might work for them, but what special design does God have for you and your ministry? We are not carbon copies but originals. We will have to answer the call, ready or not. I am disappointed in some clergy I have watched my whole life; they still need deliverance. What type of record are you leaving? God can deliver them, but they would rather enjoy the pleasures of sin and sex, and only God knows what else. Will it be worth your soul to be used by the puppet master? My God, what will be said at their funerals? It's not time to try to put people into heaven. They have lived their funeral, raggedly or richly. Will there be anybody to get saved or inspired by your shadow? Many times, the wives are left at the funerals with more questions in death than in life. It is an absolute honor when the true clergy leaves this earth or pulpit with a good name and proper provision for his wife and children **(Proverbs 31:23).** If I could say anything else about the role of a preacher's wife…it would be to let her know how much you love and respect her. Sit at her feet and gather her drops of wisdom. Tell her how much she means to you while she lives. Record her, take pictures of her, and most of all, pray for her!